The Fear
of Perfection

*Creative Strategies
for Today's
Music Director*

SALLY WAGNER

Published by
Meredith Music Publications
a division of G.W. Music, Inc.
1584 Estuary Trail, Delray Beach, Florida 33483
http://www.meredithmusic.com

MEREDITH MUSIC PUBLICATIONS and its stylized double M logo are trademarks of
MEREDITH MUSIC PUBLICATIONS, a division of G.W. Music, Inc.

Cover illustration: Alex Oakenman/Shutterstock.com
Cover and text design: Shawn Girsberger

International Standard Book Number: 978-1-57463-492-1
Cataloging-in-Publication Data is on file with the Library of Congress.
Library of Congress Control Number: 2019930023
Printed and bound in U.S.A.

23   22   21   20   19   PP   1   2   3   4   5

To music educators at every level
who are doing their best every day.

"Perfection is not attainable,
but if we chase perfection we can catch excellence."
—Vince Lombardi, Coach, Green Bay Packers

CONTENTS

ACKNOWLEDGMENTS

Sincere thanks to all who had an impact on my path as a music educator and band director. Also, thank you to those who encouraged me to share these ideas in book form. Thank you to my husband for his help, encouragement and patience. Special thanks to editor Susan Gedutis Lindsay and to Garwood Whaley, President and Founder of Meredith Music Publications, for his vision to take these chapters to a larger audience.

INTRODUCTION

When I finished my first book, *The Pursuit of Excellence: A Band Director's Guide to Success*, I found that I still had more to say. Based on ensembles I was hearing at assessments and adjudications, there were many directors who needed to be made aware of things their ensembles could improve on. I think that success is mostly about listening critically and never being satisfied. I love the Vince Lombardi quote, "Perfection is not attainable, but if we chase perfection we can catch excellence." I was rarely satisfied with the performance of my bands during rehearsals and kept raising the bar until each group was absolutely the best they could be.

This book is about continuing to chase perfection. It is organized into four sections. Part 1, Musical Excellence, shares observations, ideas, and suggestions for creating the best ensembles possible. Part 2, Professional Excellence, reminds us that while the world seems to be becoming more casual, we must not let our teaching or our approaches follow suit. Diligence and a strong work ethic will benefit students and teachers alike. Part 3, Auditioning, aims to take the mystery and stress out of auditions for both the director and the students. Part 4, Traveling with Your Ensembles, provides detailed guidance on planning for trips and festivals. We all reinvent the wheel when we travel, and I've never found anything already written to help with the process. This section shares what I learned from countless domestic and seven international trips to Bermuda, the Bahamas, England, Holland, and China. The Appendix, Quotes that Inspire, is a continuation from the first book: more inspiring quotes about excellence, persistence, achievement, and success. In my career, I found these especially helpful during times of doubt and duress.

As in *The Pursuit of Excellence*, chapters are short (except the ones on travel) and are intended to be read and pondered in small chunks. Of course, the suggestions offered are not the only way to do things; they are just ways that worked for me. It is my hope that you find within the covers some ideas to make your job easier, more successful, and less stressful.

1

Musical Excellence

Breathing Freely for the Best Possible Sound

Breathing. All day long, we take air in and let it out. We rarely think about it, but as musicians, we need to. Wind instruments and vocalists use air to transport the musical sounds they make, so an understanding of proper breathing is essential.

Focus for a moment on your breathing. It's probably slow and relaxed as you take in a moderate amount of air and release it slowly. Notice that there is no friction, just gentle in and out. Now take in a really big breath, filling your lungs all the way. Hold it for a bit. What is the natural tendency of your body? To release the air. Do so. You have just demonstrated part of Boyle's Law, normally associated with physics but at play here: Your body wants to expel the air that is built up in your filled lungs, equalizing the pressure and releasing tension inside and out.

Our challenge as wind players or singers is that we tend to apply tension to our playing or singing. Tension in our bodies is something we try to eliminate or minimize, but when we teach, we use phrases that seem to contradict this: "Firm your diaphragm," "Tighten your gut," "Push with your stomach," and "Support your breath." This language can create artificial or muscular tension and doesn't produce better sound. *More air produces better sound.* Applying too much abdominal pressure raises the tongue and closes the throat. Teachers should use language that is not misleading. The best thing to do is to speak of high notes as fast buzz and low notes as slow buzz.

The other part of Boyle's Law: the higher the pressure, the lower the flow; the lower the pressure, the higher the flow. Therefore, we want to use the minimal amount of pressure required to produce an excellent sound. A firmed trunk does not produce more beautiful sound; steady air once it goes through the lips creates beautiful sound.

Try this:

Have your ensemble take a full, deep breath, filling their lungs to 95% capacity over four conducted beats. Then, letting *all* the air release, play a predetermined note or chord together for four beats. Listen to the full resonance! By staying relaxed and using more air more freely, your ensemble will create a beautiful, warm sound.

The challenge comes when students only take in as much air as when breathing normally. We must teach them to take large, full "musician's breaths" each time while playing their instruments and release it freely. "Breathing exercises" must *only* reinforce the concept of free-flowing air, not air that is restricted in any way. In other words, don't practice forcing air out through smaller apertures to create resistance. The emphasis should be on air capacity and air flow. Be sure that students understand that lungs occupy the space from just under the collar bones to the bottom of the rib cage. That's a lot of air capacity waiting to be filled.

Arnold Jacobs, former Principal Tuba of the world-renowned Chicago Symphony Orchestra, used to say, "Air is free. Take a big breath and waste it!" Brass and woodwind players play "wind" instruments, too, so doesn't it make sense to allow *more* air to escape and not restrict its path? ■

Managing Multiple Levels in Ensemble Classes

Few other teachers or administrators in the building understand exactly what it is we do every day. Rehearsals are complex routines that change each day depending on the music we rehearse. Each piece of music presents different challenges, and choosing the appropriate music doesn't make your job easy, though it does make it more satisfying for all concerned.

If you are rehearsing an orchestra or choir, you have at least four, often five, and sometimes more parts to rehearse all at the same time. Your ears are finely tuned to hear all of them, your brain decides if they are correct, in tune, balanced, pleasant, rhythmically correct, and so on, while your body is conducting, playing piano, or both. If you are rehearsing a band, you may have to keep track of as many as eight or more separate parts, including transpositions, accidentals, varying technical demands, intonation issues between different instrument tendencies, all while communicating nonverbally with your eyes, body language, and baton.

It's sort of like asking a world languages teacher to teach French 1, Spanish 2, German 3, Japanese 2, Italian 4, and AP Russian—all in the same class. Students in music ensembles are never all at the same level. Some have questions about note names, accidentals, terminology, and pronunciation. Others ask about articulation, bowings, intonation, or difficult rhythmic figures. We isolate students who have the same part, referring to a complicated score that includes thousands of bytes of information, asking students to each perform their parts. Others wait patiently for their turn and when they are confident with their individual parts, these parts are stacked together and performed all at the same time, requiring everyone to listen not only to their own part but to other parts as well, adjusting volume, style, enunciation, articulation, balance, and more, all in an instant. It makes one's head spin to think of it, yet ensemble directors and their students do this every day.

It reminds me of a time when a school was receiving its first set of laptops. (Ancient history!) Teachers could sign up to be a recipient but had to take ten hours of class to learn to use the technology. A computer-savvy teacher who normally taught calculus and other advanced math classes was to be the instructor. He was notorious for never letting his students out of his class to attend sectionals or sports events or special meetings with college representatives, but he was a terrific teacher. In the first "class" of computer learners were teachers who had anywhere from no experience with a computer to those who had been computer literate for a few years but needed to take the class to receive the laptop.

At the first class, tension mounted because so many folks couldn't locate the power button or couldn't navigate the most basic functions. The teacher finally shouted in frustration that he couldn't deal with all the questions anymore! The band director, recognizing the situation as one she dealt with frequently, said, "John, you need to hold sectionals!" He looked up, and realization dawned at that precise moment. It was no surprise that he began to let students attend sectionals after that.

When teachers juggle the many varied demands of a rehearsal, it is imperative to remain calm, no matter how frustrating it may be. Try breaking parts down into smaller sections, working them out slowly and carefully before putting the whole back together again. Don't let the folks who are functioning at a lower level become frustrated because the group is moving too fast for them, and don't let the more advanced students become bored as you take the time to reinforce basic strategies. An optimal solution is to have those who are having difficulty attend a sectional where they can receive more thorough assistance and not feel like they're holding others back. Before and after school, during part of lunch periods, activity periods, the last five minutes of rehearsal when everyone else packs up just a bit early—these are all times that are available for intensive review or remedial assistance. Or, consider a mentoring system. Seat the more advanced students among the ones having difficulty so the high achievers can answer questions, demonstrate fingerings, and assist with articulations or vocal enunciation. Sometimes we forget what an amazing resource our students can be. It strengthens the team when students help students. ■

Creating Lifelong Consumers and Lovers of Music

One of the most important goals of music teachers should be to create a lifelong consumer, listener, or creator of music in every student who crosses the threshold of our classrooms. With the accelerated ease of accessing recorded music, the innovations in computer-generated music, and the financial difficulties of sustaining orchestras in many cities today, live music is threatened. By encouraging our students to attend local performances we can help extend the popularity of live concerts. Here are some assignment ideas that will help students grow to become the next generation of music lovers.

Music date nights

Arrange trips to live concerts. Scout out information on concerts in your area at local elementary, middle, and high schools, churches, guest artist appearances, and recitals at universities and community colleges. Ask for discounted tickets if you bring more than fifteen people. Include parents and alumni if you need more attendees. Extend the offer to faculty members, too. If everyone gets in the habit of going to concerts, it will carry over into their life beyond your program. Consider offering extra credit to students who participate or who write a summary afterwards.

Concert reports

Require a listening assignment every marking period. Have students go to a live concert and write a few paragraphs about it. Ask them to write about things you discuss in class—dynamics, articulations, style, consistency, balance, vertical precision. If they can't get to a live concert, have them listen to a CD, and write about each piece on the recording. (Requiring them to do more writing for the recorded music will encourage them to attend a live concert whenever possible!) If CDs aren't available at home, recommend the public library or start a collection of CDs you can loan to students.

Extra credit for attendance

Offer extra credit for attending concerts, master classes, or workshops on their instruments. Encourage them to respond to what they heard.

They may surprise you by commenting on things that you discuss in rehearsal.

If this seems like "one more thing to do," consider having a parent or small committee of parents take over the job. Set up an e-mail list to notify students, parents, alumni, and faculty of the dates. Create an "event" so they know how many people plan to attend. Collect ticket monies well in advance. Arrange carpools or bus transportation from the school as needed. Consider adding a dinner stop on the way to the concert for some extra enjoyment.

If these concerts turn into events that everyone looks forward to, several unexpected outcomes may occur. Ensemble bonding, student friendships, parent friendships, a chance for everyone to see the director as a person instead of only as a teacher—all positive results that can work to strengthen a program.

There's nothing quite like seeing Facebook posts from alumni who recall attending a concert long after graduation and noting how much fun it was to go to concerts while in high school. If we all work to encourage students to become lifelong lovers of music now, there's hope that live music will continue to thrive. ■

Improving Ensemble Intonation through Singing

Trying to get band students to sing in class is often so frustrating that directors just give up. Who can blame them, especially when students often haven't been asked to sing since elementary school and the young men's voices are uncertain? Still, matching pitch vocally is an important skill that allows students to hear and adjust pitch more accurately, creating better intonation in the group.

So how do we get instrumental students to buy into singing? It's important to ease into it. You might start by having everyone, after playing the last chord in a chorale, sing their pitch. When they hear the harmony the first time, they are often surprised that they were able to produce it. Make this a regular addition to your daily warmup and soon it will become second nature.

A few weeks later, try to sing a major scale together. Consider using numbers 1–8, or solfege syllables. A single syllable such as "la" also works. Concert B-flat works well for range, and percussionists can play along on mallet instruments. (*Note*: All percussionists can easily learn the B-flat scale, even if they "don't play mallets." Include them in this helpful way.)

In a few weeks, this will be comfortable so you can add the following:

Sing up the scale.

Soprano voices sustain the top note and hold the 8th scale degree.

All remaining voices descend, singing 8-7-6 and altos sustain the 6th.

Tenors and basses continue down (8-7-6)-5-4 and tenors sustain the 4th.

Basses sing the entire descending scale, stopping on 2.

Everyone sustains the ii7 chord and listens to the harmony.

Then resolve to 1-3-5-8—the B-flat major chord.

When this is comfortable, continue after the B-flat major chord and add a short chordal progression such as:

S-	8	7	8		S-	8	8	8	7	8
A-	5	5	5		A-	5	6	5	5	5
T-	3	4	3	or	T-	3	4	3	4	3
B-	1	2	1		B-	1	1	1	2	1
	I	V7	I			I	IV	I	V7	I

Because every part moves stepwise, it's not difficult for new singers to hear. From there, the sky is the limit. Consider programming instrumental pieces with singing involved, such as "Chant Rituals" by Del Borgo, or "Who Puts His Trust" by Bach, arr. Croft. As students become more relaxed about using their voices, you'll discover that the ones who couldn't match pitch well at the beginning are now doing so. And everyone is learning to listen and adjust tuning more accurately.

Being persistent pays off, and it is important for the director to sing, too. It's not about the quality of the voice; it's about the control of pitch. Working together to improve intonation is the key.

An added benefit is that once students are singing, use the sensation of the relaxed throat while singing to demonstrate the ease they are trying to achieve while playing their instruments. This technique will open and fill out most students' sound. ■

Another Technique for Building Better Ensemble Intonation

Most ensembles and their directors struggle with intonation issues. This includes professional groups; it just doesn't go away! But we can make it better. How many times have adjudicators written comments about poor intonation? How often have you stood on stage in a performance, conducting and thought "Ack! That was really out of tune!" Below is one way that might help you address this perennial problem. It's called "Island Hopping," and it's the first step toward helping the members of your ensembles listen more carefully and adjust for pitch.

Warm up enough to tune the band reasonably well. Then choose an easy chorale. Play the first note and listen to the resulting chord. Isolate the instruments that are playing the root. Have them play, tuning the unisons and octaves, perhaps using personal tuners. Listen for and eliminate the "beats"—the disruption of the sound wave caused when pitches don't quite match. When the root is really in tune, ask the students with the 5th of the chord to do the same thing. Once it is in tune, sound the root and 5th together, listening for great intonation that can easily be heard with a perfect 5th. Then add the folks with the 3rd. Tune the 3rd so that the chord sounds right and there are no "beats." (*Note*: Major thirds often seem a bit sharp and should be lowered.)

Once that is done, play the first phrase. When you arrive at the final chord of the first phrase, hold it. Isolate the root. Tune the root. Isolate the 5th and tune it. Sound the root and 5th together and tune. Add the 3rd and tune. *Voila!* You now have two "islands of good intonation." Play the next phrase and hold the final chord. Isolate and tune the root, 5th, and 3rd. Three islands! Repeat with the last chord of every phrase until the end of the chorale.

Now when you play the chorale, hold each phrase's last note until it is well in tune. Once this locks in, move on to the next phrase and do the same. Don't move on until the chord is really in tune and there are no "beats." By the time you've finished, there have been several opportunities for excellent intonation, and these remain reference points during the performance of the chorale.

Apply this to other pieces as well. Tune final chords in different sections of the pieces. Tune important cadence points. Create "islands" of good intonation. You'll soon find that as the distance between the islands decreases when you add more check points, the overall intonation throughout the entire piece improves. By focusing specifically on intonation at all of the islands, students become accustomed to listening and making necessary adjustments. Good intonation becomes a habit rather than an accident. Remember the words of Aristotle: "We are what we repeatedly do. Excellence, therefore, is not an act, but a habit." Help your students develop the habit of excellent intonation. ■

Improving Ensemble Balance

B*alance* refers to several aspects of performance:

Balanced instrumentation means having an appropriate number of performers on each instrument/voice part or rewriting parts so that missing instrumentation is not detrimental to the performance.

Balanced chords mean that all parts of the chord are heard and the chord quality is easily distinguished.

Balanced ensemble means that the melody is heard above all other parts, all parts are in proportion to their importance, and that the Pyramid of Balance is in effect at all times.

Balanced *crescendos* require special treatment to be effective.

Balanced instrumentation

A balanced instrumentation generally means that all parts are being played, and softer instruments have greater numbers to compensate for volume deficiencies. It is not unusual, in a clarinet section of fifteen, to have four players on first, five on second, and six on third because lower parts don't project as strongly as higher parts. The same is true for the trumpets. A section of nine players might have two on first, three on second, and four on third for the same reason.

Special challenges arise when there are only one or two horns, or twelve alto saxophones. The first requires careful selection of music and the later requires much softer playing or rewriting parts to reinforce other instrument groups. If the missing horns and extra saxophones are in the same band, you've got an easy solution to both issues. Have some of the saxophones play transposed horn parts.

Balanced chords

Balanced chords are critical because harmony is important to every performance. Isolating the instruments who play the root, then the 5th, then the 3rd allows everyone to hear all the chord tones. This is an essential technique when polychordal writing is used. Each group must be able to relate to the other members of their chord in order for the effect to be as the composer intended. Again, isolate the two chords, tune them, and finally play them together so that each is the same volume. Make certain that the 3rd of each chord is in tune so the listener knows whether the chord is major or minor in the fleeting moment before it passes to another chord.

Balanced ensembles

Balanced ensembles have two challenges: making certain the melody is always easily identified by the listener, even as it is passed among different instruments with varying volume characteristics, and keeping the bass voice stronger than the tenor, which is stronger than the alto, which is stronger than the soprano. Because instrumentation is often backwards (more musicians playing higher instruments and fewer on the lower ones) adjustments in dynamics are necessary.

First, the melody. Consider having your ensemble perform a piece from the beginning, but only playing when they have the melody. (Drop out when the part changes to an accompaniment or harmonic part.) Hear it pass from instrument to instrument, and hear it change volume as it is picked up by lower instruments or flutes and clarinets in lower registers. Make adjustments so that the "presence" of the melody is always the same. Play the melodic parts with the bass line. Then go back and add all the other parts, keeping them in proportion at a lesser volume. Can you always hear the melody? Are the static or repeated rhythmic parts covering up part or all of the melodic material? Is percussion too loud? Make adjustments again so that the balance is as it should be.

Proportion is essential in putting together all the voices of the ensemble. Now that everyone can identify the melody and which instruments parts play it at any given moment, focus on the Pyramid of Balance. This will enhance your ensemble sound, making it fuller, richer, and warmer. Be sure the bass is prominent. Require that your lower instrumentalists play with their fullest sound. Because low voices don't project as strongly, air needs to be more energized. Short notes, especially, need to have more volume or they get lost in the overall ensemble sound. Keep the soprano voices in check, perhaps at a softer dynamic than what is written, especially if you have a plethora of flutes and clarinets or violins. Recording your ensemble will allow you to listen objectively to balance and proportion.

Balancing crescendos and diminuendos

Balancing crescendos and diminuendos is a special challenge. Again, it's based on the physics of each instrument. A clarinet crescendo is much less effective than one played by a tenor saxophone, but that doesn't mean it can't be balanced. The clarinetist gives a more dramatic increase while the tenor saxophonist is more subtle, perhaps starting even more softly than marked but only growing partway in volume. A way to check: the chord should sound the same at both ends of the crescendo or decrescendo. Try playing the chord or note softly, then grow. Balanced? In proportion? Now reverse, loud first, then soft. Balanced? In proportion? Now that this technique is learned, it can be easily applied and reminded.

Creating all the layers of balance in your ensemble will surely result in a better sounding group. However, be warned that it is not a one-time lesson. Rather, it needs to be reinforced and required for every piece of music. As your students become more aware of balance and how they must adjust to achieve it, your job will change from teaching them to merely reminding them.

An analogy: Imagine making a batch of chocolate chip cookies. Ingredients are: chocolate chips, flour, sugar, eggs, butter, vanilla, salt, baking soda. Imagine putting them all together in equal amounts—2 cups of chips, 2 cups of flour, 2 cups of sugar, 2 cups of eggs, 2 cups of butter (so far, not too bad!), 2 cups of vanilla, 2 cups of salt, 2 cups of baking soda. The cookies would taste very strongly of salt and vanilla and have a gritty baking soda texture. Music is the same. The ingredients of the piece (melody, harmony, rhythmic accompaniment, bass line, percussion, etc.) must be added together in the proper proportion to ensure a delightful outcome. Students must recognize when they have the melody (chocolate chips) and bring it out. When they have the harmony, bass line, or accompaniment (dough) they must reduce their presence a bit, and even less when they are the vanilla or baking soda. As the salt, they are important but perhaps not to the point of being present all the time. Taking the time to create a balance of ingredients in your ensemble will guarantee a much better performance with all parts in proportion. ■

Reinforcing Rhythmic Accuracy

Rhythm is a critical element in all music. It contributes to vertical alignment so that all notes that appear on a certain beat happen exactly at the same moment. It provides pulse and forward movement and allows the audience to relate to the music in a primal manner: feet tapping, heart pounding, or body swaying.

Students associate with rhythms, especially if the beat is interesting or syncopated. Rhythm speaks in a current musical language that youth recognize and appreciate. In fact, many contemporary songs don't even use melody, as "beats" are entertaining on their own.

If rhythm is so critically important, why is it, then, that so many ensembles perform with inaccuracy? It's doubtful that they do it intentionally, but there's an element of discipline missing that is so obvious to educated listeners that it requires special attention.

When groups sight read, there is more of an emphasis on counting the rhythms to assist in playing the piece correctly. Unfortunately, as the piece becomes more familiar, the tendency is to "know how it goes" and not count anymore.

A truly fine, disciplined ensemble continues not only to count, but to divide and subdivide to ensure the highest level of rhythmic accuracy. Vertical precision is essential to fine performances, and the slower the tempo, the more important subdividing becomes.

To assist students with this concept, consider using an amplified metronome set to play eighth notes during the slow parts of your daily warmup. Getting students accustomed to hearing the 1+2+3+4+ every day will reinforce their ability to continue the silent counting in their brain. Directors can also remind them that they, the director, are counting, dividing, and subdividing every measure, even though they are probably much more familiar with the pieces than the students.

Rhythmic accuracy is something all students can achieve. No matter how inexperienced or advanced they are as players, this is within their control. Directors must remind and reinforce it daily because students, being students, will lapse into moments of laziness or forgetfulness. Once counting is an established habit, the dividends in the performances will be right on beat! ■

A Stress-Free Approach to Improving Sight Reading Skills

Judging sight reading is an eye-opening experience. There are as many different approaches as there are directors, and some are more successful than others. Here's one approach that works well and takes the stress out of sight reading new pieces for both the director *and* the students.

During score study:

▶ Use your time and look through the entire piece. Check for repeats, dynamic changes, tempo changes, and key signatures.

▶ Look for accidentals, odd articulations, and phrasing.

▶ Take a moment to skim the program notes so you know a bit about the piece.

▶ Check the percussion parts for instrumentation, and decide on substitutions.

▶ Decide upon the tempo(s).

During the time to assign percussion parts and tune the timpani:

▶ Try to assign everyone to a part, even if it means sharing (i.e., triangle and suspended cymbal on the same part can be performed by two students if you have a lot of percussionists).

▶ It is important to try to involve everyone.

▶ If there are extra students, have them stand beside the performers to help them. Too often percussionists don't look up while reading, so the extra folks can watch the conductor and count aloud quietly.

▶ Consider putting an extra person on the other octave of a xylophone or marimba using softer mallets.

During the time with the ensemble:

▶ For about a minute, talk about the "big picture": repeats, D.S.'s, and time or key signature changes.

▶ As you talk about each aspect, have students physically touch the page where these are. Tactile learning is real.

- ▶ Give a very brief overview of the piece—why it was written, specific style(s), and anything relating to something you've performed before.

- ▶ Use the remainder of the time to finger through and "speak" the piece. By saying and fingering the rhythms, the students will have "played" the piece, and you have the opportunity to talk above their voices with statements such as: "Trumpets, you have the melody here," and "Low brass—softer here," or "Clarinets—I can't hear you. Bring it out!"

Then give a *performance* of the piece including phrasing and, if possible, stylistic nuance. By practicing this method on everything new that is played in class (including lines from the method book or technical studies), students will become proficient at the process, and sight reading will be a comfortable experience for all. ■

100 Life Skills and Qualities Taught or Reinforced Through Instrumental Music

Accepting compliments
Accepting criticism
Accountability
Appreciation of others
Arts appreciation
Assertiveness
Attentive listening
Breaking tasks into manageable parts
Collaboration
Commitment
Communication
Compassion
Comprehension
Concentration
Conceptualizing
Confidence
Conflict resolution
Consistency
Cooperation
Coordination
Courage
Creative thinking
Creativity
Decision making
Decoding
Dedication
Dependability
Discipline
Emotional response
Emotional development
Empathy
Encoding
Flexibility
Focus
Following multistep instructions
Following nonverbal communication
Following verbal directions
Friendship

Goal setting
Good sportsmanship
Happiness
High expectations
Humility
Imagination
Language development
Improved reading tracking
Improved respiration
Individuality
Information processing
Innovation
Integrity
Intellectual curiosity
Intuition
Language development
Leadership
Literacy
Logical reasoning
Mathematics of rhythm
Memorization
Memory
Mentoring
Motor skills
Neurological multitasking
Organization
Patience
Pattern recognition
Perseverance
Persistence
Pride
Problem-solving
Promoting happiness in yourself
Promoting happiness in others
Proportion
Questioning
Reading
Reading comprehension

Reduces stage fright
Reliability
Resourcefulness
Respect
Responsibility
Risk acceptance
Risk-taking
Salesmanship
Satisfaction in a job well-done
Self-esteem
Self-expression
Self-management
Sense of achievement
Sharing

Social skills
Spatial intelligence
Stress relief
Taking turns
Teamwork
Time management
Tracking (visual)
Trust
Understanding historical periods
Understanding political influences
Using symbols and languages
Value judgements
Verbal recall proficiency
Work ethic: strong! ■

Preventing Teacher Burnout through Careful Pacing

Proper pacing improves both learning and teaching. It comes into play in several categories, including the following:

Lesson planning

When determining what you'll be rehearsing on a given day, be sure to allow time for brief breaks in your group's playing. Constantly having a mouthpiece mashed into their face can cause fatigue that can lead to bad habits. Breaks can be used to provide a short explanation of the back story of a piece or the composer, stylistic references, or anything else that is relevant. Breaks don't need to be long—maybe thirty seconds to a minute, to allow muscles and blood flow to return to normal before being assailed again. If you save your talking for the middle of rehearsal instead of at the beginning, students can start playing right away (which is why they signed up for band!)

Marching rehearsals

Be sure to plan breaks in your marching rehearsal schedule, especially if you're outside or the weather is hot or humid. Directors are often the ones putting out the least exertion and they can forget how hard and how constantly the students are working. "Take it back and run it again! Go!" means that while the director stands still and thinks about what (s)he just saw, students are running into place with great spirit and energy. Water breaks and time to stand still or sit in the shade are important parts of rehearsals. They shouldn't be overlooked.

Change

When taking over a program, whether it is your first job or not, be aware of changing too much too soon. What you inherit may not be anything like what you envision, but changing everything at once can result in failure and frustration for both you and the students. Be aware, also, that there may exist a strong feeling of loyalty for the way things were done before you arrived. Changing everything causes an emotional upheaval for the students and perhaps some resistance to your new ideas. Prioritize! Decide which element will have the greatest impact, and make changes there first.

Extracurricular activities

There are two parts to this one: what you expect your students to do and what you are taking on for yourself. Solo & Ensemble Festival, Jazz Band, Pep Band, Clarinet Choir, Flute Choir, Brass Quintet, Trombone Quartet, Tuba Choir, Flags, Winter Guard—the list of wonderful educational experiences goes on. But how much can you ask your top students to add to their busy academic and athletic schedules? Help them prioritize so that they maximize their learning and participation without burning out and dropping out.

As for you, trying to be everything to everyone is noble and impressive but often leads to stress and a feeling of being overwhelmed. Learn to delegate. Is there another faculty member whose background and experience allows them to coach Winter Guard? Was an English teacher a flute major for a while, and is he or she willing to coach the flute choir? Are there experienced parents who share your vision and are willing to help? What about training a student conductor to rehearse Pep Band? Limiting after school activities to two or three days per week means you can go home twice a week or get school work done at school, freeing your evenings. Set up a rotating schedule that allows you to focus on one group each day, rather than running from group to group and not really being helpful to anyone.

Let's assume you have all of the groups mentioned above. Here's an example of a schedule where you stay for ninety minutes after school three days a week. The ensembles in bold font are coached by you:

▶ Mondays–**Jazz Band,** Flute Choir (with faculty coach), Tuba/ Euphonium Choir (with faculty or university coach). On the second Monday of the month, Jazz Band takes twenty minutes to work alone while you check out the Flute Choir. On the fourth Monday, same, while you check out the heavy metal.

▶ Wednesdays–**Pep Band,** Winter Guard (with parent coach), Clarinet Choir (with local university student coach). On the second Wednesday, Pep Band runs through stand tunes with the student director/drum major while you check out the Winter Guard. On the fourth Wednesday, check in on the Clarinets. Arrange to meet with the university student briefly after each rehearsal.

▶ **Thursdays–Solo & Ensemble participants,** Brass Quintet, Trombone **Quartet, Flags**. Schedule the S&E participants for ten-minute coaching sessions with you. Brass Quintet and Trombones can each sign up for two consecutive slots for focused coaching with you but will work independently the rest of the time. Check in on the flags (coached by flag captain) at the end to see their routine.

It may also be possible to trade occasionally with one of the other coaches. For example, the Tuba/Euphonium Choir coach also happens to be the bass player in a local combo. Let him/her take the Jazz Band once in a while and you take the Tuba/Euphonium Choir.

Options for finding coaches:

▶ faculty at your school

▶ university students nearby

▶ colleagues at nearby schools (perhaps an exchange!)

▶ retired master teachers in your area

▶ parents experienced in an area you require

▶ older siblings/alums who participated in the groups before

▶ Skype coaching (small ensembles) with private teachers

Planning for pacing is an important element of running a successful and varied program . . . one that allows the director occasional time off! ▪

Teaching Students to Practice Effectively

Practice makes perfect. We have heard this phrase so many times and most of us believe it. But think about it: If we practice it, but practice it incorrectly, does that make it perfect? Of course not. In fact, the better line is "Practice Makes Permanent." What we practice and *how* we practice has a huge effect on how we perform. Take this example: A student practices a tricky part ten times. The first nine, he has problems and doesn't quite get it correct. The tenth time, however, is perfect so he puts his instrument away, satisfied that he finally got it right. But what are the chances of playing it correctly the next time? They are one-in-ten at best.

The correct way to practice is to start a tricky passage so slowly that it is impossible to make a mistake, then gradually speed it up until the correct tempo is reached—and always repeating it if there was an error. Consider this: A famous soloist practices with a row of ten pennies on his stand. Each time he plays a challenging spot perfectly, one penny gets moved to the other side of the stand. The goal is ten perfect repetitions. However, if he makes a mistake, all the pennies go back to the start and he beings again. Ten perfect performances is perhaps a bit much to ask of younger players, but even three or five pennies can assist students to practice slowly and correctly rather than "learning" mistakes that will have to be unlearned later. Just imagine how much more fun practicing would be if pennies were replaced with chocolate kisses!

There's a great tee-shirt quote that says, "A good musician practices until (s)he gets it right. A great musician practices until (s)he *can't* get it wrong." This is a wonderful inspiration for correct practice. It has also been quoted as follows: "An amateur practices until he can do everything right, and a professional practices until he can't do anything wrong."

Whichever way we present it to our students, they must be encouraged to practice correctly, however slowly that must be, instead of learning mistakes and hoping it will come out better tomorrow. A consideration for rehearsals: It is always fun and exciting to show students how fast a piece will eventually go by playing quickly through it before it has been carefully learned. This can challenge students to work harder. However, don't forget that each fast run-through is teaching some students to play incorrectly, and those mistakes will need to be unlearned and the correct way relearned.

Even if many students in the ensemble are capable of playing at the faster tempo, be sure to occasionally play at a much slower tempo to reinforce correct playing for the students who are a bit behind. Once the correct fingerings have been learned by all students, increasing the tempo becomes a much easier job with greater outcomes. ■

Suggested Programming Strategies

Concert programming is a perennial challenge for all directors. Here are some suggested programming ideas that can provide variety and a pleasing concert experience for your audience, as well as a varied learning experience for your bands. First and foremost, ensure that the music fits your ensemble. Well-chosen music highlights the strengths of the group and disguises or minimizes their weaknesses. Be sure you have strong soloists to showcase when the music requires it. **The pieces suggested here may not be the best choices for your ensemble and are only meant as examples.** Aim for about thirty minutes of music or less, which allows time for announcements and applause. If the concerts will have an intermission, put the longest half first to keep the audience interested.

Advanced ensembles

Seven-piece program:		
Opener (Fanfare or short, zippy piece)	Also Sprach Zarathustra—Strauss	1:20
Serious piece (multi-movement?)	2-3 mvts. from Vaughan Williams Folk Song Suite	6:00
Slow piece for contrast	Benediction—Stevens	3:30
March	Belgian Parachutistes—Leemans	2:50
2nd serious piece, but shorter	Country Gardens—Grainger	2:15
Something popular (or recognizable)	Shenandoah—Ticheli	6:45
Closer (exciting, fast and fun)	Sweet Trombone Rag—Sweet	2:50
		22.40
Six-piece program:		
Opener (Fanfare or short, zippy piece)	La Peri Fanfare—Dumas/Longfield	1:50
Serious piece (multi-movement?)	3 mvts. from Giles Farnaby Suite—Jacob	5:00
Slow piece for contrast	O Nata Lux—Forbes	3:00

Something popular or recognizable	Loch Lomond—Ticheli	6:30
Serious piece	Solas Ané—Hazo	4:30
March	Prestissimo!—King, arr. Swearingen	2:00
		22:50

Five-piece program:		
Opener	American Barndance—Saucedo	3:50
Serious piece	Madrigalum—Sparke	4:00
Slow piece for contrast	Amazing Grace arr. Himes	3:30
March	American Salute—Gould/Wagner	5:00
Closer (fun)	Disney at the Movies—Higgins	3:30
		19:50

Four-piece program:		
Opener	Fanfare for the Common Man—Copland/ Longfield	3:13
Serious piece	First or Second Suite in F—Holst	11:30
Something popular, recognizable, or slow	Nimrod—Elgar/ Reed	3:00
March	They're Off!—Jewell	1:30
		19:13

Three-piece program:		
Opener	A Tameside Overture—Sparke	8:00
Serious piece	Symphonic Dance #3: Fiesta—Williams	6:50
March/Closer	They Shall Run and Be Free—Karrick	6:20
		21:10

When choosing an intermediate band program, remember that about twenty minutes of music is plenty for a concert, especially if there are other groups performing. Bands that can handle more advanced programs than these could certainly play for longer but be sure to plan accordingly to prevent fatigue—both of the performers and the audience. Intermediate ensembles should ideally perform for a shorter length of time, so these programs that follow are shorter.

Intermediate ensembles

Five-piece program:		
Opener	Soaring!—Morales	2:20
Serious piece	Loch Lomond—Ticheli	6:30
March	Crown of Castile—Vinson	2:35
2nd serious piece but shorter	Fortis	3:00
Something popular or recognizable	America the Beautiful/Swearingen	2:15
		16:40

Five-piece program:		
Opener	Peregrin: A Traveler's Tale—Akey	4:30
Serious piece	Earl of Oxford's March—Byrd/Williams	2:30
Something popular or recognizable	Eternal Father—Edmondson	3:00
2nd serious piece	Lost Lady Found—Grainger/Sweeney	3:00
March	Pathfinder's March—Sparke	2:00
		15:00

Four-piece program:		
Opener	Fanfare Americana—Hosay	1:50
Serious piece	Earthdance—Sweeney	6:40
Contrasting piece	Psalm 42—Hazo	2:20
Closer	That Old Hound Dog Rag—Standridge	3:50
		14:40

Four-piece program:		
Opener	Reverberations—Balmages	3:00
Serious piece	Korean Folk Song Medley—Ployhar	3:30
Contrasting piece	Hymnsong of Philip Bliss—Holsinger	5:00
Closing piece	Arabian Dances—Barrett	3:00
		14:30

Three-piece program:		
Opening piece	Ancient Dialog—Burns	4:00
Contrasting piece	Yorkshire Ballad—Barnes	3:00
Closing piece	Rites of Tamburo—Smith	4:00
		11:00

Three-piece program:		
Opening piece	Scenes fr. an Ocean Voyage—Balmages	5:30
Contrasting piece	Horkstow Grange—Grainger/Sweeney	2:20
Closing piece	Russian Sailor's Dance—Gliere/Vinson	3:00
		10:50

For younger or less experienced groups, putting a fun piece at the end adds energy at a time in the concert when they may be starting to wear down. It also helps to end the performance with a lively piece that encourages hearty applause.

Also consider themed concerts, especially for the end of the year. For example, a concert entitled "That's Entertainment!" might include a sports selection, a cartoon or kids show theme from television, a medley from a Broadway musical, a computer game theme, and selections from a movie soundtrack. A concert entitled "Under the Sea" could include ocean-related songs ("Songs of Sailor and Sea" by Smith, "Scenes from an Ocean Voyage" by Balmages, "Sea Songs" by Vaughan Williams, Selections from *Pirates of the Caribbean* and "Under the Sea" by Moss, from the Disney movie). Decorations are simple (16mm film banners, old movie projectors, TVs and computer screens made from construction paper, or fish hanging on the wall, and crepe paper "seaweed" hanging from above the stage). Guest appearances by football "stars" in jerseys, cartoon characters (The Simpsons are particularly easy), mermaids, whales, and pirates can also add a festive element. Invite students from feeder or nearby schools to maximize the fun and the impact.

A particularly entertaining concert featured a middle school band performing for about twenty-five minutes. During the time before the concert, when parents dropped of the students and had a while to wait, a slide show of first-grade photos of each of the eighth grade band members was shown on the wall behind the band setup.

Another was called "Postcards from Boston" and followed a high school band trip to a festival there. Pieces in the concert highlighted activities the group participated in while there: a medley from *Phantom of the Opera* because they had seen the musical, a sketch featuring Lycra-masked Blue Men including a PVC "drumbone" made by one of the band dads, "Witch Hunt of 1692" by Grice marking their sightseeing in Salem . . . you get the idea.

Other ideas might be a New Orleans–based concert ("Dance of the Harlequins" by Clark, "At a Dixieland Jazz Funeral" by Spears, "Hurricane!" by Fagen, "High Water Mark: The Third Day" by Sweeney, etc.) or one to honor veterans and servicemen and women ("Marches of the Armed Forces" by Sweeney, "Missing Man" by Johansson, "American Salute" by Gould, "This Is My Country" arranged by Brubaker). Another fun idea is to do a time machine concert and travel back in time to different styles of music from medieval ("Of Dark Lords and Ancient Kings" by Barrett, "Pange Lingua" arranged by Conley) to Renaissance ("Canzona Bergamasca" by Scheidt, arranged by Daehn, "Renaissance Suite" by Susato, arranged by Curnow) and up through Classical, Romantic, ragtime, jazz, etc.

By selecting a wide variety of music from different periods, we enable students to learn to play in many different styles. It's important to choose music that is educationally sound for most of the year, but there is certainly nothing wrong with easing up for the end of the year or a pops concert. Be creative. Allow your audience to be entertained by the variety and scope of your ensembles' abilities, and don't forget to program something fun or familiar into the mix.

An end-of-the-year massed band/combined bands selection is fun and impressive if your school has more than one band. Consider playing one or two pieces together, perhaps having one of the selections be something the less advanced band played during the year. Use caution choosing the pieces so that you don't overprogram for the younger or less experienced band. Reaching a bit is fine, but all students should be able to find success. Be sure to allow ample rehearsal time for the less experienced band to learn the more difficult piece. Remember: It's not how difficult the music is; it's how successfully and beautifully it's played that impresses the audience.

Giving adequate thought to the programming of your concerts will keep audiences coming back for more. ■

Mastering the Fine Art of Silence

Composers use the many options at their disposal—dynamics, articulations, tempi, and style—to create contrast in their music. Perhaps the most obvious, though, is the one that directors use least: silence. It is silence that sets the stage for sound. Leopold Stowkowski said, "A painter paints pictures on canvas. But a musician paints their pictures on silence." Let's look at the places where silence can become an integral part of an ensemble performance.

> ▶ **Phrase endings.** Because we are accustomed to "looking ahead," we may neglect to let a phrase end properly. Supporting the sound to the end of the written duration, gulping a breath, and moving quickly into the next phrase creates unease for the listener and the performers. The music must be allowed to take a breath along with the musicians. Consider this: At the end of significant phrases, conduct a proper release then allow the musicians to take a full breath before cueing the next entrance. Breathe with them! The duration of the breath is dictated by the tempo of the piece but there's not a huge rush, especially at slower tempi. The many releases and re-entries in chorales provide multiple opportunities to practice this. Breathing together in tempo on the pickups and memorizing the first notes will help ensure that entrances begin together.

> ▶ **Section endings.** It is especially important to let the last chord or sound resonate at the end of sections. Allowing a collective "sigh" or breath to take a moment's space, especially before a tempo change or new material, will enable the audience to process what they've just heard before a mental shifting of gears. Don't be in a hurry to move on. Caress the last note and let its sound resonate out into the performance space. Remember that it takes a while for the sound to dissipate in the hall. Savor the brief moment of silence before going on.

> ▶ **Fermatas.** Fermatas and grand pauses are often used at ends of sections or for dramatic moments. Don't be afraid to increase the drama by drawing them out a bit, then adding a moment of silence after the fermata so the sound can float on the air, dissolving into total silence before moving on.

▶ **Screaming rests.** There are moments in some pieces where the composer has written a rest, perhaps a very brief one, for all members of the ensemble, either for the impact that a quick moment of silence will bring or as a prelude to a dramatic chord that follows. Whatever the reason, these rests must be approached exactly the same by all members of the ensemble. Conductors must decide if the note before the rest will be released suddenly, with a taper, or with a bit of an accent. Selecting the "articulation" of the rest will make the silence distinctive and more effective. It's almost as if the sudden, unexpected moment of silence "screams" out to the audience, creating a dramatic contrast to the sounds immediately preceding and following.

When listening to a program of even the most beautifully performed music, a listener must surely appreciate a moment of silence as the ultimate contrast to continuous sound. Allowing the audience a moment to process and enjoy only takes a second yet greatly enhances the experience.

Whether slow and lyrical or fast and rhythmic, rests are an integral part of making music enjoyable to listen to. They are like the negative spaces in art. Skilled painters let a bit of bare canvas show through or create shadows to allow the main subject to appear more prominently. Likewise, as you prepare your music, remember the importance of silence as a way to emphasize sound.

Perhaps it is no coincidence that the words "silent" and "listen" are made up of the same letters. ■

Crescendos: Maximizing Their Effect on Music

They are subtle yet powerful: the little *cresc.* strategically placed in the exciting moments of a composition or the < marking under the notes in dramatic moments of a piece of music. There are also several other ways that the crescendo can be used to enhance the expressive nature of your performance. Consider:

- ▶ **Before a key change.** Accidentals mean that the composer is modulating, or using a chord substitution to make the music more interesting. Moving toward those pitches with a crescendo—leaning into them, if you will—helps the audience recognize more fully the harmonic and melodic changes. Accidentals are a place where intonation tends to suffer, so be sure the accidental is in tune. Isolate the chords, then put them back together slowly before returning to regular tempo, allowing musicians to "hear" what is going on so they can expect it and make it more engaging.

- ▶ **Moving from unison to harmony.** Another place that the crescendo has great importance is when parts go from unison to harmony. Imagine the trumpet section all playing in unison. Then, at a certain point, they break into three-part harmony. The volume of the trumpet section will be cut to a third of the unison volume. Therefore, all the trumpets must know where the divide happens and crescendo into the harmonic moment. Otherwise, their part all but disappears into the texture of the ensemble, with the lower parts being even more likely to disappear. This also applies to clarinets. Nine clarinets playing in unison have one volume. Nine clarinets playing three on a part in harmony have a very different volume, so adjustments must be made. Crescendo into the place where the unison divides into harmony so the presence of the section is not diminished. Apply the same technique to horns and trombones or any instrument with multiple parts.

Balancing the crescendo

Due to the physics of sound and the acoustical properties of some instruments, everyone making a crescendo of the same amount will result in an unbalanced peak. Adjustments must be made to allow the lower frequency instruments to make a larger change and the louder or more direct instruments to make a somewhat subtle change. To demonstrate this, ask your saxophone section to play a chord at *mp* then, in four beats, crescendo to *ff*. Ask the clarinet section to do the same. Have both groups of instruments do it together. Can you really hear all of the clarinet parts? The stronger instruments cover the softer instruments, and the higher pitches project more strongly than the lower pitches. All members of the ensemble must learn and remember the acoustical properties of their instrument in its different ranges so they can make the adjustments necessary to blend and balance every chord at all dynamic levels and in all ranges. Directors can help by listening *through* the chords, not just *to* the chords for all the pitches in the correct proportion to ensure the highest quality performance possible. ◼

Decrescendos: How Soft? How Gradual? When to Begin?

Like the crescendo, performing an effective decrescendo presents challenges of its own. How much softer? How gradual? When should it begin?

Let's start with the definition.

Decrescendo: "a gradually reducing force or loudness; diminuendo" (www.dictionary.com) or "a gradual decrease in volume of a musical passage" (Merriam-Webster). (*Decrescendo* and *diminuendo* are synonymous.)

Consider that this involves two concepts: reducing intensity and decibel level (flow of air). How do we help our students create beautiful yet easily performed decrescendi? First of all, are they running out of air naturally? If so, the decrescendo occurs naturally. If they are not running out of air, then encouraging them to relax and play more calmly will create an effective softening of tone, both in intensity and in volume.

As in a section crescendo going from unison to divisi passages, when players reverse from a divisi section to a unison passage, a decrescendo must be inserted. Working as a team to create a softer unison tone is essential for remaining balanced within the ensemble.

If we expel our air evenly and fully, a natural decrescendo occurs as we run out of air. No special physical control is needed. By just blowing naturally, the descrescendo is gradual and effective. If we relax, we allow the air to calmly release and the natural decrescendo occurs. What could be simpler!

Balancing a decrescendo is critical, too. Due to the physics of the different instruments, adjustments must be made so that individual instrument sounds don't dominate the balance as the ensemble softens. Practice playing a balanced ensemble chord at the dynamic level of *f*. Now soften to *p* over four counts (or however many) and listen to the chord at the end. Is it similarly balanced? Are all parts audible? Is it soft enough? Repeat and reinforce often. By understanding the acoustical properties of their instruments, students will learn to make these adjustments on their own, using their listening skills to evaluate their success. ■

Diagnostic Listening to Improve Your Ensemble

While adjudicating festivals it is shocking to see how many conductors don't seem to be conducting the ensemble sitting in front of them. It is confusing for judges and audiences alike to watch the grandiose arm movements and expressions of sheer joy and ecstasy on the director's face while hearing plodding attempts by the students to perform music that is obviously not as well prepared as it should be. In these cases, it would seem that the director is not conducting the actual ensemble, but rather the recording that (s)he used as a reference.

As a director, it is important to have the final "sound" of the pieces in your head but only if it doesn't replace the actual sound of your ensemble. It is the job of the director to choose music that is challenging yet attainable and that shows off the strengths of the ensemble while disguising any weakness or missing instrumentation. It is also the job of the director to hear where the group is starting and plot a plan to take the players to the level of achievement required for public performance. Listening to scholarly recordings helps define a possible endpoint, and there are so many that are accessible on YouTube and elsewhere in the internet that students should be guided toward the recordings that you, the director, feel are of the highest quality. Hoping your group will get better is not sufficient. You must be their GPS and guide them to the final product.

Recognizing and addressing the existing problems in your ensemble is key. Attend to intonation. Teach solutions for rhythmic inaccuracies. Adjust balance. Let everyone know where the melody is and how to adjust dynamics so that it floats on top of all the other parts. Encourage good tone, expressive playing, use of dynamics and articulations, as well as consistency in all of these things. Every rehearsal should be carefully planned to cover specific elements of the pieces being prepared. Don't just keep playing the pieces over and over hoping they'll get better. Perfection of all parts and the whole is the goal.

Record your rehearsals and listen, comparing what you hear from your ensemble to the professional recordings you've been listening to. Then make your list of performance goals for the next rehearsal. Persist until you get your own group to sound as much as possible like the reference recording you've selected. Don't allow yourself to think "It's close enough" or "Not bad for middle school." Every day, work toward your goals, making incremental improvements but not giving up until the highest quality performance is reached.

When you take the stage, look each student squarely in the eye and smile, knowing that what you accomplished was a team effort. Then proudly conduct the ensemble that sits on the stage in front of you. ■

Developing a Skillful, Versatile, and Engaged Percussion Section

They're all the way in the back of the room and easily out of our sight-lines. They are sometimes inattentive, somewhat confused, and often hunting for equipment that was not put back in its place—but they are so important to the overall success of your group that you must pay them their due attention.

If you have drummers who say "I play snare" but avoid timpani, bells, and xylophone, consider training them to become well-rounded percussion-ists. These versatile musicians are the ones who can truly enhance your ensemble. They are proficient on all the instruments and know the proper way to play them. They can get several different tones out of a triangle and are not afraid to tackle a melodic mallet part. With any luck, at least one of your players has some piano experience and can help teach the others.

Percussionists will rarely walk in your door with skills on mallet instru-ments, but it is well worth your time to teach them. If you have the option of an occasional pull-out sectional rehearsal, show them how to play all the instruments and the accessories. Let them experiment. Insist that only percussionists play percussion instruments just as only euphonium players play the euphoniums. Band, after all, is not a petting zoo for curious musi-cians. Once they have learned the finer points of playing tambourine, sleigh bells, flexi-tone, and the rest, they will have a new appreciation for just how dynamic their position is in the ensemble.

Teach them to tune the timpani. Post the ranges of the kettles nearby (available, by brand, on the internet). Provide a pitch pipe or other pitch source and suggest that they tune by starting with the heel of the pedal all the way down and tune up to the required pitch. If they have trouble, show them that by placing their finger lightly in the center of the head, they will silence some of the overtones, making it easier to hear the fundamental pitch of the kettle. Allow plenty of time for them to do this in class, even if the ensemble must wait. Have them work in teams at first to build confi-dence. There is safety in numbers, after all.

In rehearsal, take time to listen to how they fit into the overall fabric of the ensemble. Are they too loud? Too soft? Using the correct mallets for the sound you desire? Are they struggling with something that you can help with? By incorporating them into every part of your rehearsal, you'll keep them engaged and they will feel like a part of the ensemble rather than mere accompaniment.

Include percussion (hopefully everyone on mallets) in the warmup. Usually there are scales and slow harmonies or chorales, and mallet players can figure out how to participate fully. If not, take them aside and show them the patterns for mallet scales. They'll soon have them all memorized, far ahead of the rest of the class. If you have only bells and xylophone, have two players on each instrument and take turns so more can have the experience.

Before a performance, ask the percussionists to look behind them and evaluate how their sounds will interact with whatever is there. Is it a cinder block wall that will amplify their sounds? Is it a thick curtain that will absorb some of their sound? Is it an acoustical shell that will project their sound more strongly into the audience? Knowing what is behind them and being able to adjust their volume accordingly will allow all the parts of the ensemble to be heard, not just the percussion. Be sure to listen for their balance once the performance starts, and give them an indication of whether they are loud, soft, or right on target.

With very little effort, percussionists can overpower the entire ensemble. Timpani alone, or suspended cymbal rolls, are loud enough to cover tuba pitches or trumpet harmonies. There are certainly times when the percussion section can rise up out of the fabric of the band for solo lines or introductions, but a well-taught section will then return to the balanced ensemble sound.

Challenging the percussion section to recognize the melody and which instruments are playing it keeps them involved and thinking. They need to be aware, for example, that accompanying clarinets requires softer dynamics than accompanying low brass. They must be alert to the changes required by the music.

Reverberation is also a consideration in percussion. Timpani and low toms initiate a lot of low rumble. Consider muting the tom heads using commercially available gel mutes, felt squares, or a wallet on the head, and try several different mallets/sticks to determine the appropriate sound. Articulated timpani solos will sound clearer with harder mallets but rolls are more even-sounding with softer ones.

One last thought: The composer included certain instruments in the composition for a reason. Try to use all of the special instruments to give the best representation of the composer's intent. If you don't have the instruments, borrow or rent them. Otherwise, program pieces that have percussion instruments that are available at your school. ■

Teaching Students What "In Tune" Sounds Like

The battle rages on: Use individual tuners and really zero in on intonation problems, or *don't* use tuners because no one will ever learn to play in tune if they are relying on a crutch.

I vote for tuners. Here's why:

Most students don't know what *in tune* sounds like. Perhaps they play an instrument where the sound is far away from their ears, such as a euphonium, tuba, trombone, French horn, clarinet, low clarinet, saxophone, low saxophone, oboe, or bassoon. Even if they play flute or trumpet, it's not always easy to hear their own sound in the large ensemble. Hearing the sound is critical to discerning intonation, and if they can't hear themselves, any effort toward adjustment is wasted. How many elementary students spend time tuning before class? Until they have developed a consistent sound, it makes little sense to tune each player. String players have a much different situation, often relying on their teachers to tune their instruments at each class. As they grow, their pitches are right there—just inches from their ear, making it easier to hear intonation problems if they occur.

Some teachers attach a clip-on tuner to each music stand for use by the students. (These work well for oboes, clarinets, trumpets, and trombones and are easily visible when clipped on the bell.) Others use clear shoe bags with tuners and pickups stored in each pocket. (These tuners work well for flutes, saxophones, low clarinets, euphoniums and tubas.) Still others require each student to purchase their own tuner, the one that works best for their instrument. Most tuners now have a range of five to seven octaves and respond quickly as notes change. Using a tuner while going through a warm-up routine offers a visual confirmation that one is in or out of tune and how to adjust. Using a tuner that is clipped directly onto the instrument (the tuner or the one with the pickup) will help eliminate bleed from other instruments. Tuners with pickups clip onto the bell of the instrument and the tuner sits on the music stand in clear view. Tuner apps work for at-home practice but not in a group setting, as they tend to pick up surrounding instruments as well.

Many argue that being tied to A=440 every day seems unrealistic because temperature and humidity changes create problems for maintaining a reliable pitch point. However, students with perfect pitch are thankful that the pitch remains constant day to day, as it minimizes problems they might otherwise experience, and other students learn to react in a consistent way to notes that are generally out of tune.

Using a tuner for at-home practice is also beneficial to the overall intonation of an ensemble. When parts are played softly, pitch often dips. Tuners make this immediately apparent for correction. Notes in the extreme upper and lower registers of instruments often require adjustment. By repeatedly referencing the tuner, students learn to adjust for pitch tendencies and anticipate problem spots.

Once everyone has learned where their pitch problems lie and how much correction is needed, ensembles will sound much better in tune and students will begin to hear and adjust on their own. At this point, the tuner becomes a tool for warmup and occasional use only.

Three hints for tuning:

1. If a student knows they are out of tune but isn't sure which way to adjust, have him or her choose a direction and make the adjustment. There is a 50/50 chance of making the right choice. If they made the wrong choice, there is now a 100% chance of making the correct one!

2. Tune from below the pitch. It is always easier to hear the pitch when approaching it from below. Flatten the desired note with an embouchure adjustment, then bring it up to the correct pitch. This exercise helps students begin to hear small differentiations in pitch and allows them to practice slight embouchure adjustments for use later.

3. When tuning timpani, put the pedal all the way down with the heel and bring it up to pitch. It's easier to hear when you've arrived and is more likely to stay at that pitch than if the head is tight then loosened to match pitch. Are there too many overtones to hear an accurate pitch? Place a finger gently in the very center of the head. Now tune. Many of the extra harmonics have been dampened and the fundamental is easier to hear.

After years of hearing judges' criticism of intonation in the upper wood-winds or inner parts, I discovered that tuner use by all wind musicians quickly solved the problem. By using a tuner to learn when they are out of tune and what they need to do to correct it, students begin to learn what "in tune" sounds like and they experience how pleasing it sounds to play with good intonation. ■

Using Warm Air to Advantage When Beginning a Sound

W hy is it that, at the beginning of a piece or a section, some notes speak right away when we play them and others start a millisecond late? Especially for brass players but for woodwinds as well, it is a challenge to control exactly when a note begins. (Percussionists, vocalists and strings don't have the same problem, so their sound begins on time and the rest of the ensemble comes in a microsecond later. *Oops!*)

This happens in part because the temperature of the air inside the instrument is different from the temperature of the air being used to start the tone. When warm air meets cool air, what happens? In the earth's atmosphere, it's called a tropical depression, a hurricane, or a tornado. In band, the result is a tiny delay in the initiation of sound. Fortunately, there's an easy fix.

Before beginning, blow a little warm air into your instrument. If the air inside is warm already, then adding warm air from outside—a buzz (brass), reed vibration (woodwinds), or air column vibration (flute)—will allow the sound to start much more precisely. The same thing must be repeated after four or more measures of rest as instruments cool quickly, especially flutes. Reeds must be moist in order to vibrate. Long rests can be problematic if players do not pay attention to this.

A wonderful side effect of blowing warm air into the instrument is that it will improve intonation, because when instruments have been resting and then come back in, pitch is sometimes low until the instrument is warmed up again.

To get the entire ensemble to initiate sound securely and at the same moment, have everyone breathe together, in tempo, one beat (or more) before the piece begins. If everyone has the first note or first few notes memorized, all eyes can be on the conductor and the beginning note will pop. If the piece is slow, following this routine is even more important, as is counting, dividing, and subdividing the preparatory beat(s). A successful beginning, in which all enter at the same moment, captures listeners' attention immediately.

Here is a quick and very easy exercise to practice:

1. Hold a bright green tennis ball in your hand for all to see.

2. As you toss it into the air, have students breathe in.

3. As you catch it in your hand, students say "toe" (or "tah" or whatever syllable you use). Repeat several times.

4. Next, use instruments on any given pitch. (Put warm air inside the instruments before you begin!)

5. Toss the ball into the air and catch it again.

6. Students breathe in on the toss and begin the note as the ball lands in your hand.

7. Then, substitute your baton stroke for the motion of the ball.

This approach yields immediate results, but you'll need to keep reinforcing it. Consider creating a special cue to remind groups introduce warm air into their instruments before they enter, so that you won't have to stop to verbally remind them. Any time an entrance is not together or out of tune, however, stop and repeat the entrance in order to reinforce good habits. ■

Establishing and Maintaining Trust

Trust is like a silk strand spun by a tiny worm. It can be stretched into fiber so strong it can support many hundreds of pounds, but once broken, the fiber is almost impossible to repair in a way that makes it as beautiful and strong as it once was.

Consider how trust applies in the band room.

The director trusts that:

- ▶ students will take care of the instruments they've been assigned
- ▶ students will bring their "A game" every day and practice at home
- ▶ students will show respect in class and outside of school
- ▶ students will responsibly dispose of their "water," old reeds, tissues, etc.
- ▶ students and their parents will commit to the excellence of the team

The students trust that:

- ▶ the director won't let them embarrass themselves in a performance
- ▶ the director will give them good advice regarding playing their music
- ▶ the director will respect them and not insult them in front of their peers
- ▶ the director will choose appropriate music that they can perform well
- ▶ the director is committed to the excellence of the team

The parents trust that:

- ▶ their children will be treated fairly in class
- ▶ their children will be respectfully treated by their teacher
- ▶ their children will be safe while in the care of the director
- ▶ the director will apprise them of any problem before it becomes serious
- ▶ the commitment to the team will be a great experience for their children

This list is by no means complete, but rather a sampling of the importance of trust in the music classroom.

Band, orchestra, or choir is a class that students take for multiple years, and the director is often the same for several years. As the relationship of trust evolves, each party—director, student, and parent—is responsible for maintaining their portion of that relationship. Failure in any aspect stretches the thread of trust to the breaking point. You don't want that thread to break! Trust must not be assumed but rather demonstrated and reinforced to students as well as parents.

Each party must assume complete and individual responsibility to maintain the delicate balance of honesty, courtesy, kindness, and respect that trust demands. If you wonder whether an action might be inappropriate or interpreted the wrong way, don't do it. It's not worth risking the comfort of the trusting relationship. Once that thread is broken, it will take many years to repair, and even after it is repaired, it will likely be laced with doubt and never quite as strong as before. ■

Ten Common Mistakes to Avoid at Assessments

1. **Tuning on stage.** Tune in the warmup room. Tuning on stage usually highlights problems rather than solving them. That said, if there is a piccolo or soprano sax joining in later in the program, by all means take a moment to tune. If you notice a problem during the warmup selection, fix it—but going down the line of flutes or saxes in front of the judges is not a good plan.

2. **Playing a long warmup selection.** It only takes a few minutes to get the ensemble focused and ready to perform their adjudicated pieces. Why waste chops, focus, and tone quality on a long warm-up? A piece that is several levels easier than your festival selections can do the job just as well without tiring the students. A three-minute (or less!) march or chorale works as well as or better than a drawn-out piece—*and* your students will arrive at the end of your adjudication with better intonation, more endurance, and more energy.

3. **Never playing softly.** Any good band can play loudly, but it takes a *great* band to play softly with a great sound and good intonation. Ask your students to practice something softly for one minute each day, using a good sound and enough air. It can be the Birthday Song, something they have made up, a lullaby, something from their music—it really doesn't matter. We spend so much time at the other end of the dynamic spectrum, and being able to soothe the ears of the audience with beautiful *pp*'s and *p*'s creates amazing contrasts and control in your music selections. To help students understand what *pp* should sound like, have one player on each part play a section of the music softly. Instruct the other students to listen for its clarity, lightness, and transparency. Then add the next player on each part, striving to achieve the same lightness and transparency. Continue adding players until all are included. Review this technique frequently until *p* and *pp* become part of the group's musical vocabulary.

4. **Starting crescendos too soon.** It has been said that a crescendo should be the shape of a trumpet bell—a long part where there is little change and then a dramatic flare of sound at the end. So many

groups begin the crescendo as soon as the notation appears. Often, this results in a crescendo that reaches its dynamic goal way before the ending, causing a loss of dramatic effect at the least or an over-blown, out-of-control, edgy loudness at the worst. Hold back a bit so that the most change occurs toward the peak of the crescendo.

5. **Not being consistent with dynamics throughout the piece.** There are often several forte markings in a piece of music. The ensemble should plan to do one of two things: either perform the fortes all at the same dynamic level each time they appear, or work for a slight growth in level as each subsequent *forte* appears, creating more excitement as the piece continues. (*Note*: The latter works better for pieces with recurring thematic material all marked *f*.) Often, the first forte is too loud, making it impossible for the coming fortissimo to reach its full impact and still maintain a good sound. Forte should only be a bit stronger than mezzo forte, not the loudest your students can play! "*Merely* forte" is an easy way to convey this to your musicians. The performance will be greatly enhanced by holding back a bit so that the climax of the piece will be more exciting and more in control.

6. **Not allowing the melody to be clearly heard at all times.** Have you ever rehearsed a piece and asked the students to play only when they have the melody, dropping out when they have other mate-rial? This can yield some amusing results, especially when the clari-nets or trumpets play the whole time, figuring they always have the melody. Also, it is instructive for students to hear the melody fade and resurface as it is played by louder and softer instruments that have not made the necessary balance adjustments. It's a great exer-cise to allow students to hear how the melody is passed among the different instruments. Next, consider having students only play when they have the accompaniment. The volume of this is often enlightening—way too much accompaniment for the volume of the melody. The audience only hears the piece once, so they must have no doubt what the melody is. Allow it to float on top of the accom-paniment parts even if it means minor adjustments to dynamics of the melodic and/or nonmelodic parts.

7. **Not understanding the physics of the instruments.** It takes approximately twenty clarinets to match the volume of one trumpet. Most bands do not carry a twenty-to-one ratio, so something else has to happen. When clarinets have the melody marked *mf* and brass have accompaniment parts also marked *mf*, the brass need to adjust to play a bit softer while the clarinets may need to adjust to play more strongly. If trombones have a unison melody that suddenly breaks into three-part harmony, their dynamic level suddenly drops by two-thirds, so adjustments must be made in order for all parts to be heard. At first, this information will likely need to be dictated by the director but eventually students will begin to focus on what is going on around them and make some of the adjustments themselves. Likewise, higher instruments project more loudly than lower instruments, so low brass and low woodwinds with melodic material will need to raise their dynamic level. If there is a descending line, this is especially important or the end of the descent will fade to almost nothing. Sometimes the lowest instruments in each section will need to play slightly shorter values on very low notes so they will be heard. Energized air will help this, too. Also, the piccolo must often play much softer than notated and end a tiny bit early as the high sound lingers after the band has released the chord.

8. **Unleashing the percussion section**. Percussion instruments can easily play the loudest with the least effort. In fact, one suspended cymbal roll, with a crescendo, can obliterate the entire middle of the band, saxes and trumpets included! An overzealous bass drummer eliminates any pitches tuba or timpani might be adding. Crash cymbals, frequently played as though it were a 150-piece band, overpower all other sound for a second or more. Newer music often includes percussion as an equal partner with brass and woodwinds, allowing solo sections or occasions when the percussion parts can rise up out of the fabric of the band to add an exciting element.

The problems arise when the section does not return to the well-balanced ensemble sound afterwards or plays too loudly for the size of the band. Teach your percussion section to listen for the clarinets. If they can't hear them, they're probably too loud. Ask your percussion section which instrument(s) they are playing with at certain times. Do they know? Can they sing the melody at various places in the music? If not, they are most likely too loud to hear the others. When performing, listen for the percussion section and give them guidance when they need to play more softly or strongly, especially in a venue to which they are not accustomed.

One more word for percussionists: Before performing, look behind you. Is there an acoustical shell or cinder-block wall? If so, parts may need to be played more quietly than in your band room. Is there a heavy plush curtain? Some sounds may be absorbed, so watch your conductor for signs of needed adjustments. Also, be certain that *all* percussion instruments and music stands are placed between the player and the director so that everyone can see the director at all times. Chimes are especially problematic in this regard, as they are often placed so that the player has his or her back to the conductor.

9. **Not playing in proportion.** So many bands seem to treat dynamics and balance as "extras" that don't really affect the overall performance. This is far from the truth; hearing the melody clearly at all times is critical. If there is a countermelody, it is likely to be second in importance. The bass line is next, with static rhythmic or harmonic accompaniment coming after. Percussion, depending on its role in the music (supporting or equal partner with brass and woodwinds), is either last or somewhere in the middle.

Teaching each musician to understand their role at every point in the musical selection is important to the overall balance and proportion of the music. It is also necessary to remember that instrumentation is often reversed from what the Pyramid of Balance tells us: a larger percentage of lower voices are needed and a smaller percentage of higher voices. Encouraging the bass voices to provide a strong foundation will improve the overall sound quality of the ensemble.

10. **Not understanding the nature of the music.** Too many times music being performed is not understood by the conductor. If it is originally a vocal piece, why is the ensemble playing such loud and heavy dynamics? If it is a composition based on a folk song, why are folks breathing in the middle of "words"? These elements are the responsibility of the director. Be sure to carefully read the program notes or look up information about the piece online. Know something about the composer and other pieces (s)he has written.

All styles of music are not equally loud, and do not utilize dynamic levels from 1 to 10. Some only use 1 to 4, with 4 indicating forte but not intended to be screaming at the audience. Directors can get carried away with the power of their ensembles and want to show it as often as possible. This causes an audience to shut down and stop listening because everything is so loud. Composers use dynamics as chefs use condiments: a sprinkle here, a dash there. Don't make your pieces sound as if they are entirely covered in mushroom gravy! ■

2

Professional Excellence

Awards and Recognition

Many music programs offer awards to recognize outstanding student musicians. This has been an important part of maintaining and growing pride and ownership in a music program since the days when the John Phillip Sousa Award was the only one available. Then, organizations started making a variety of certificate awards available, followed by pins and trophies for all sorts of noteworthy accomplishments. These tokens of appreciation are important ways to reward your best students for their dedication, hard work, service, and achievements. Pins and engraved trophies and plaques are great if you can afford them. If not, printing certificates on fancy paper gets the point across. A combination of both may be the ultimate solution.

The following categories of awards might be useful in recognizing the leaders in your program as well as those who contribute in other essential ways:

- **Outstanding Musicianship Award**. The best performer in your top ensemble.

- **Most Valuable Member Award.** Can be one for each ensemble. Qualifications vary: leadership, attitude, service, strong musician, etc.

- **Most Improved.** Again, one for each ensemble. Consider having this one voted on by members of the ensemble. Maybe nominations are made first. Be sure to keep this from becoming a popularity contest, and consider using written ballots.

- **Outstanding Section Leader.** Leadership is a valuable trait that should be recognized publicly.

- **Superior Rating, Solo or Ensemble**. If you have students who participate in Solo & Ensemble Festival.

- **Excellent Rating, Solo or Ensemble**. Same as above. Also consider additional recognition for Superior and Excellent ratings at the district or state level.

- **All-State, All-District, All-County Honor Bands**. Participation deserves recognition.

▶ **Chamber Ensemble Awards.** For the Brass Quintet, Woodwind Quintet, Clarinet Choir, Jazz Band, Pep Band, Flute Choir, Brass Choir, etc. Acknowledge the students who give extra time to your program, especially if they are not receiving class credit for their time and efforts.

    ▶ **Outstanding Band Parents.** A certificate and public recognition is always appreciated, as is a gift card. Consider having something personalized for the parents who help you throughout the year; note pads or mugs with the band's name or a slogan are useful possibilities. Be sure to recognize, in a special way, any individuals who have gone above and beyond.

    ▶ **Student Directors, Drum Majors, Band Officer Awards, Four-Year Participation Awards.** Recognize these unique leadership contributions.

    ▶ **Special Awards.** Student winners of solo competitions, student accompanists, section leader, or squad leader recognition.

There are more categories that may apply to your program. Don't hesitate to give recognition where real effort was given. Be careful not to award mediocrity, however, as that will likely diminish the relevance of all awards.

True story: A parent once commented that one reason his son stayed in band all four years, despite scheduling difficulties and the need to take summer school to open a spot in his schedule, was that every time he participated in something extra he received recognition. The student had also been a part of drama tech crews and never received anything for the many hours he devoted to after-school rehearsals. He eventually lost interest in drama. This was an introverted student who appreciated being noticed. The band award he received each year? Solo & Ensemble Participation.

The Music Stand catalog once posted a quote that sums it up well: "Awards are not given for a single act of greatness, but instead are the recognition of all the hard work that preceded it." Recognizing acts of dedication, achievement, and service will boost morale and encourage students to work even harder, knowing that they will be appreciated and rewarded for their efforts. ∎

The Importance of Being Organized

F ew things are more important to developing an award-winning program than being organized. Here are some examples of aspects that need to be carefully thought out and planned:

▶ **Inventory**. As the director, you are responsible for cataloging (by serial number) the instruments assigned to your care. It is also important that you keep repair and maintenance records for each instrument, noting each repair done and the date, as well as records of chem-cleans, bow rehairing, string replacement, and overhauls. At some point, continuing to repair an older instrument may become less cost-effective than purchasing a new one. Computer databases make this task manageable.

▶ **Uniforms**. Know what you have and when it was last cleaned or replaced. Keeping accurate records will require marking each piece with a cataloging number (possibly on the tag). By including the year of purchase and the number of the clothing article or part (such as "18-24," for parts purchased in 2018, number 24), replacement of older parts will become easier.

▶ **Achievement**. Consider tracking achievement for each student. There are several ways to do this, including programs like SmartMusic, proficiency tests, etc. Help each student create performance goals and work toward them by completing sequenced steps of learning along the way. Some ensembles use a ranking system for this; students complete certain skills to achieve "4th Class Musician" ranking, different skills for "3rd Class," etc., with awards or other acknowledgement given for each level conquered.

▶ **Sequential learning**. It is critical that you develop an orderly learning plan for your ensembles. This includes selection of appropriate music for each performance throughout the year and teaching the required skills sequentially and at a pace that allows *all* students to succeed. For example, expecting your brass students to learn to double-tongue in a few weeks is unreasonable. Introducing the concept at the beginning of the year and including some exercises during daily warmups while encouraging students to practice it at home will likely yield a better result over time. Similarly, learning to create four-measure phrases without breathing in the middle does not happen quickly. Include chorales in the daily warmups and insist that students breathe anywhere other than on the bar lines unless marked. Repeat the phrase any time you hear someone breathe in a musically disrupting way. Over time, breathing between four-measure phrases will become automatic.

▶ **Daily lesson plans.** Either written or well-thought-out plans will maximize your rehearsal time. Record rehearsals and listen during your drive home. This allows you to evaluate what was successful and what still needs more work before you meet the class again. Rather than standing in front of the group and wondering, "What should we play first today?" be prepared! Know what you need to accomplish and summarize what still needs work at the end of rehearsal, so students know what to practice at home.

▶ **Scheduled performances**. Get these on the school calendar at the start of school or before. (Some school auditoriums are so heavily booked that getting the concert dates entered for the next year is done before the end of the previous one.) Inform parents and students as soon as dates are known. This will reduce date conflicts. Some school systems insist upon a thirty-day notice for any required events. Today's lifestyles are so much more complicated than even ten years ago, so do yourself and your ensemble parents a favor and get the dates settled and posted a minimum of three months prior. Try to post dates for the entire year because spring semester is often busier with sports teams, club events, science fairs, AP testing, etc. Having your dates on the calendar first will ensure full participation, especially if you avoid the other important dates.

▶ **Warmup routine**. If your class starts the same way every day, students will know what to do without being told. This saves time and allows you to begin class promptly. For example, if every class begins with a breathing exercise and the pieces to be rehearsed are listed on the board, students have only one priority—getting to their seats on time with instruments and required music. If the beginning of the warmup is performed to a metronome, the director is somewhat free to set the metronome running and take care of minor instrument repairs (loose spring, stuck mouthpiece, etc.) during this time, though repairs ideally should be brought to your attention before school or another time of the day when you have time to address them. Once class is started, protect your rehearsal time by staying focused on the entire class, not one student with a malfunctioning instrument. One rehearsal minute spent on a repair is more like fifty-plus minutes of instruction lost—one minute for each member of the class!

▶ **Rehearsal techniques**. Everyone is different and, as conductors and teachers, we must play to their strengths, but you will teach more efficiently if daily expectations are consistent. Meeting students at the door and saying, "I have grading to do today so you can just sit and talk" establishes an expectation that rehearsals are not a priority. It also lets students know that not fully participating once in a while is probably okay. The standard of excellence, once set, must not be compromised. Each rehearsal is critical and well-planned. Each student is expected to practice until their part is polished. Everyone, including the director, gives their best effort every day. Excellence is a habit. Get grades done at home, before or after school or during planning time.

▶ **Pull-outs or sectionals**. Plan ahead for a month at a time to be sure each group gets equal time and that classroom teachers are aware of the upcoming impact on their classes. Include a second time option for students who may have a conflict or are not allowed out of a particular class. When these schedules are handled at the last minute, attendance is more likely to be spotty.

Establishing the understanding that every rehearsal matters greatly will go a long way toward eliminating a host of problems and delays. If one student didn't remember to bring a repair to you before school and has to sit out the rehearsal, have them finger along so that they are learning. "I forgot my instrument today" cannot become an excuse to sit in the back of the room and finish homework for another class. Time spent in your classroom must always be spent learning the music. By being organized yourself, you can demand a high level of planning and preparedness from your students. If you're lackadaisical, you can't expect them to be any different, no matter how hard you try.

Remember: If you're not focused, it's frustrating for them. If students see your class as a waste of time or time better spent elsewhere, you'll lose numbers each year. Spending time before class to be sure you have a plan for the rehearsal will reap huge benefits. Also, parents who see that you are organized and efficient will be more willing to offer their time to help. No one has time to fritter away their days, least of all a successful ensemble director. ■

Commissioning: How to Proceed and What to Expect

Having a work commissioned for your ensemble is a tremendous educational experience for students, director, school, parents, and community. If you've never done this, be assured that it is not as difficult as you might think. Here's a list of what you need to know:

- ▶ It often takes three to five years for a composer to complete a work once it has been contracted.
- ▶ The timeframe depends the number of commissions in the queue before he/she gets to yours.
- ▶ The cost will be between $2,000 and $10,000, depending on the difficulty, length, etc.
- ▶ Consider combining with a group of directors from other schools to save money.
- ▶ Choosing a very popular composer often means more money and more time needed.
- ▶ You can choose what kind of composition you want: chorale, march, overture, etc.
- ▶ You can choose how long you'd like the piece to be. (Ballpark: $1,000 per minute.)
- ▶ You can choose to dedicate the piece however you want.

Consider several inexpensive ways to raise monies for a commissioning:

- ▶ Collect donations to commission for a special occasion, like the fiftieth anniversary of the school or the principal's thirty-fifth year at the school. Collect donations at concerts and have a designated parent collect donations before or after school, maybe on the first day of each month.
- ▶ Hold schoolwide fairs and sell tickets to events such as a faculty dunking machine or Pie in Your Face for $1 ("Duck for a Buck"— whipped cream pies being tossed at seated faculty). These activities are inexpensive and fun.

- ► Hold a faculty talent show and charge for tickets. Sell your commissioning idea and ask for donations, too.

- ► Host a ticketed family movie night at the school auditorium. You could even repeat it, with something like, "Fourth Friday Movies." Sell popcorn!

- ► Hold a flea market. Collect and sell donated items. Rent booth space for those who want to sell their own things.

While raising the money, contact a few composers and find out what kind of a schedule they are on and how much the piece you have in mind will cost. Make your decision and let the composer know. Take care of the contract as soon as possible. That gets you on the list! Some composers will want a 50% deposit. Be prepared for this.

If money is an issue, consider hiring a composition student at a nearby university, or the composition professor. Choosing locally means that the composer may be more available to come work with your ensemble.

Once the piece is received, practice it well. Consider paying to have the composer attend the last rehearsal of the ensemble. Or perhaps have him or her attend the "World Premiere" of the piece. Be sure to announce the composer and have them stand at the concert.

Having a work commissioned for a special occasion is very worthwhile. Having a piece commissioned for something recurring, like alumni band or the anniversary-of-the-school concert every five years, is even better! The piece gets played more and people come to expect its performance, giving it even more value. ■

Keeping Success in Perspective

The band scores high marks at an assessment or festival, maybe even taking first prize!

A student or students get top marks at a solo festival or with a duet or trio!

The marching band finally has the highest score in the competition!

The choir is chosen for a highly visible performance at a special event!

The director is recognized for outstanding achievement by members of the community!

These are all wonderful accomplishments and everyone should be very excited when they occur. However, problems arise when students, directors, or parents let success overcome propriety, common courtesy, or the actual truth. Here are some thoughts on keeping it all in perspective:

▶ There are many national-level festivals for bands, orchestras, and choirs to attend. Earning first place at any one of these does not mean you are the best in the country. Not every band in the country was represented. However, you took first place at a national-level festival, which is wonderful! Just keep the announcement accurate.

▶ Students who earn Superior ratings for solos or chamber ensembles or who win solo competitions have every right to be proud. However, holding up a Superior rating to groups that did not score as high is bad manners. Winners should learn to be supportive of other students who also participated and not gloat about their own success.

▶ Marching competitions take all forms. A high score one week might be replaced by a moderate score at the following week's event. Be happy but be courteous of the other groups, too.

▶ Choir members, don't brag to the band and orchestra members that *your* group was selected, not *theirs*. Wait for the others to congratulate you. This encourages teamwork and appreciation rather than jealousy and rivalry in the department.

▶ Directors work hard and often long hours. To be recognized is a wonderful thing but wearing an "I'm a winner!" tee-shirt to school is definitely not recommended. This was your turn. Others will have their turn. Again, teamwork over conceit.

▶ School ensemble auditions bring on a lot of stress. Prepare your students for the audition process. Remind them that once the seating is posted, they should be aware that some people will be very happy but others may feel disappointed or let down based on how their audition went. Be sensitive to both groups. Excessive cheering and fist pumping will only make matters worse for the folks who didn't get the seat they'd hoped for. You're all still part of the same band!

As teachers, it is important to remind students to be kind, courteous, and mannerly. Hard feelings are difficult to erase and unnecessary to foster. We may be very successful at what we do but, as a person, we are no better than anyone else. By making others feel better about themselves, the feeling is returned to us. ■

Dressing for Success and Why It Matters

As students walk into your room each day, they see you and form an impression. Are you lounging by your desk, coffee mug in hand, reading the paper? Are you straightening chairs for the rehearsal? Are you writing on the board? Are you on your cell phone? Are you not in the room at all? Each of these scenarios makes a visual impression on your students, setting their expectations. Conflict arises when they see a relaxed, detached individual that then stands up and starts yelling for students to hurry up and get into their seats.

Modeling is hugely important in teaching. Every day you are being judged by your students based on how you look, how you dress, how you react, how you talk, how prepared you seem, how focused you are—the list goes on. Consider these:

▶ You dress in jeans and a hoodie to "blend in" with the students and become "one of them."

▶ You wear shorts and a polo with flip flops because it's hot out and you'd rather be at the beach.

▶ You felt like crap when you woke up so you dressed in sweats and considered wearing your slippers to school.

Then consider these:

▶ You wear professional clothes to show students that you value your education and the opportunity to show that education can elevate them.

▶ You wear a lightweight shirt, open at the collar, and khakis because it's hot out, and though you'd rather be at the beach, you don't want to sweat all day at school.

▶ You felt like crap when you woke up so you wear a nice skirt and blouse and spend extra time on your hair and makeup, hoping it will improve your day.

There is research connecting students' casual attitude toward education with the casual attire worn by teachers. In her book *Mind What You Wear,* Professor Karen J. Pine cites many examples of "enclothed cognition" research showing that how you dress not only has an effect on the performance of those who see us but also *how well we perform our jobs*. It's a quick read and well worth it, especially if you feel you aren't getting the respect you deserve in your classroom or that your students have a very casual attitude about learning. Improving the impression you make and the quality of the job that you do is worth the few minutes spent planning your wardrobe for the day. ■

Fundraising and Keeping Track of Money

When school budgets shrink but music programs grow, fundraising is usually the most effective way to continue providing the best instruments, repairs, and materials for your students. There are many companies available to help you raise money but consider a few things before deciding which way to go.

▶ How much profit do you make per item? $.50 per $1 candy bar seems like a great margin but how much candy can you sell and how frequently? Selling 2,000 bars earns about $1,000. If your school has 600 students, can you sell more than 2,000 bars?

▶ How often will you be able to hold the sale? Wrapping paper is great and everybody needs it but how much can one use in a year? Consider a fundraising item that people run out of, or one that is edible.

▶ Are you considering products that appeal to kids as well as adults? Kids don't buy candles or wrapping paper or wreaths, and adults don't generally buy chocolate bars or lollypops. Choose your fundraiser to fit your community.

▶ Consider seasonal sales. Cheesecakes and pies sell well before Thanksgiving and Christmas and, like wreaths and poinsettias, can bring $5–10 profit per unit, and folks will want to buy these things every year. Beach towels imprinted with your school mascot or logo will sell in the spring and may have some repeat business but perhaps every other year is a better strategy for that kind of item. Alternate it with Passover/Easter cakes and pies or quiches, and you may have a winning combination.

▶ Food always sells. Pizza kits, cookie dough, coffee cakes, breakfast items, cheesecakes, pies, cupcakes, citrus fruit, apples, nuts, and the like have a returning customer base. Depending on the item, purchasers must pick up frozen foods on the day of delivery so items can be taken home to the freezer. Careful planning and clear communication will take care of this. Have a plan for what to do with any items that aren't picked up. (Cafeteria freezer?)

Having money at your disposal for repairs, new music, replacing instruments, special performers, and guest speakers allows freedom to enhance your program and enrich your students' musical experiences. A worthwhile goal is to become almost entirely self-supporting. Since school budgets will probably not increase significantly, create a plan to recondition or replace instruments and equipment gradually. Expect your school or school system to contribute one or several new instruments each year, but realize that for a band of fifty, it may take ten to fifteen years to replace the inventory. By planning ahead you can be sure you have sufficient funds to keep your program running smoothly.

Keeping track of money

- ▶ It's always a good idea to have several parent volunteers on hand whenever money is being collected. Find out how your bookkeeper wants checks written and what goes on the *Memo* line.

- ▶ How does (s)he want coins turned in: rolled or changed into bills?

- ▶ Count all money at the end of the event. This goes for fundraising, concerts, and all other times that money is collected. Have several people count the same money to ensure accuracy. Make sure all bills face the same direction. Bundle bills by denomination: $20s, $10s, $5s, etc.

- ▶ Consider buying a calculator that prints a receipt. When turning in piles of checks, bookkeepers often want two matching copies of a tally done on a calculator or adding machine. Tally checks in bundles of $1,000–$2,000 and place a paper clip or rubber band around them. Include the two copies of the tally. Make the job as easy as possible for the school bookkeeper.

- ▶ A locking safe is helpful if there is no access to a drop box for evening events at school. Under no circumstances should you take money home to count it. Lock it up securely at school and count it the next day or, better yet, have parent volunteers come in to count. The more you can separate yourself from the actual money handling, the better off you are, just in case a discrepancy occurs.

▶ If you're collecting money for a fundraiser that is to be used toward a trip, consider whether you are putting all the money into one "pile" to decrease the amount that each student pays or whether each student is earning money for their own "account" to pay for their trip. Three-copy receipt books are especially helpful for the latter. (Refer to *Part 4, Traveling with Your Ensemble* for more detail.)

▶ Check and double check all deposits. There are several easy computer programs available to help you keep track. Find out what the bookkeeper uses—QuickBooks or similar—and consider getting the same. It is critical that all money that goes through your office is correctly and quickly accounted for. At the end of each month, ask the bookkeeper for a printout of your financial activity. Check your records against this and be sure it's accurate. Do this at the end of the school year as well. Taking thirty minutes at the end of each month to catch problems, oversights, or mistakes may save you money and headaches later on. ■

Don't Give Up on Any Student

S he's the worst 8th grade flute player ever to audition, I thought. She'll never be able to keep up with even the least experienced band. She has a sound that will never blend. Her rhythmic sense is awful; it will be like having to start over at the beginning. Why accept such a bad flute player when there are so many decent ones? She'll never feel successful. It is so tempting . . .

All of these thoughts followed an audition by an 8th grader coming into the program. I considered how easy it would be for her to get "lost in the cracks" of scheduling between 8th grade and 9th grade . . .

Then the phone call came. A current band parent, who was also a Girl Scout leader for this child, called to beg. "Please watch out for her. She won't have any friends at the high school. She's very shy. She's from a very small private school with not much of a band program."

So the student went into the lowest level of band, where she would have the opportunity to catch up. Early in the year she agreed to switch instruments—to bassoon, because her long, double-jointed fingers were more suited to that instrument. Her parents agreed that she could take lessons.

Three weeks later, the private teacher called. "Have you heard her play? She's a natural!" It was almost impossible for me to believe this was the same musician. Bassoon seemed to be the perfect instrument for her, and because she had less difficulty fingering the notes, her rhythm improved greatly. With the help of the guidance counselor, she got rescheduled for the next higher band because it met when she had lunch—an easy switch.

At the end of the year when auditions were held for the following year, she auditioned into the top band, an ensemble that predominantly performed the most difficult music at an advanced level. In the fall, she auditioned for All-State Band and made it—three years in a row! Senior year she was principal bassoon in All-State Orchestra and got to play an important contrabassoon solo in the concert. Her parents bought her a bassoon so she could continue to play in college.

It's not fair to judge how far a child can progress before they are even given a chance. It's not possible to predict who will rise to the occasion and surpass all expectations. It is a music educator's job to teach *everyone*—to take them from where they are to where they can possibly go, accepting that some are merely enjoying the time spent playing, some are competitive, some are driven, some are gifted, and not all will be great musicians. It is not up to us to say who gets the opportunity to excel. It's our job to provide the best opportunities possible to *all* of our students with the hope that each will discover what they're capable of achieving.

Lesson learned. ■

Some Things to Think About When Everything Is Going Well

Finally! Everything is running smoothly. You've established yourself as a successful teacher and are pleased, most days, with the results you're getting. The school is a good fit for you and the paycheck is welcome every two weeks. What could be better! This is when you finally have time to stop and take a look around you. What shape is your inventory in? Will you have enough uniform parts and concert attire for the anticipated growth of your ensembles next year?

Planning ahead can help you avoid huge budget requests that may not be met. Consider the following plans:

Purchase a few new instruments each year. Few schools can afford to replace all their tubas in one year. Most replace a few each year. Plan for the long haul—should you buy more instruments of a lesser quality or focus on one or two really good quality ones? Perhaps a combination of the two—one top-of-the-line instrument and a few lesser quality ones for "at home" practice. Have a rotation in mind—woodwinds, brass, percussion—so that you don't end up short. Check your repair records. There may be instruments that are becoming very expensive to keep in working order. It may be more prudent to replace them than to keep repairing them. Higher quality instruments tend to last longer than the less expensive varieties that are flooding the school markets.

Purchase the best quality possible for your advanced group. Older instruments in good working order can be rotated to the intermediate group or relegated to "at home" status for extended use. Maintaining and cleaning school instruments is *critical* to their longevity, so be sure to teach students to clean them regularly. Create a four-year rotation for chemical cleanings to really get brass instruments clean. Do the same with overhauls for woodwinds. Remember to budget for replacement heads for the percussion equipment. Though the heads may look like they're in good condition, they should be replaced every two to three years for maximum performance quality. Consider having percussion students purchase their own stick/mallet bags to reduce school cost. Schools can provide beaters/mallets for the large instruments such as chimes, bass drum, gong, etc. Stringed instrument bows should be re-haired at regular intervals, and the climbing cost of string replacement every year or two must not be overlooked.

Put uniform parts on a replacement rotation. Marching band uniforms are generally replaced all at the same time so the colors match and the styles can be updated. If it is your job to raise the money, this requires setting aside funds each year until the total is accumulated. Fundraisers, admissions, donations etc., work well if it is an ongoing process. Remind the principal of the uniform renewal date so that the school can (hopefully) contribute.

If the school or board of education has the responsibility of replacing the marching band uniforms, be sure to give them a few years' notice that your time is coming. Ordering takes time, as does making room in the budget for a large expense. Concert attire that is not part of the marching uniforms will need to be replaced or supplemented as well, preferably on a rotating basis rather than all at once. Purchase pants one year, jackets another, accessories on yet another. If possible, ask students to purchase part of the uniform (maybe shirts or skirts) so the school can provide blouses for the ladies and the pants or tuxedos for growing guys who will need a different size each year.

New music perusal. Listening to the new music publications is essential for staying up to date on new compositions and arrangements available for your ensembles. Listen while commuting or designate quiet time to focus on what you're hearing, but be sure to spend time making informed decisions about what your ensembles will prepare for performance next year.

What can you delegate?

When everything is running like clockwork, take a look around to determine if there are tasks you can delegate to others to allow yourself time to do the musical extras that parents and students generally can't help with. It is important to protect yourself from being overworked, stressed, or burned out. Can you delegate some responsibilities to parents that would allow you to lighten your load a bit?

Consider these areas where others might contribute:

▶ counting money and preparing deposits
▶ numbering the new uniform parts (use the year and then the cataloging number (18-50 for something purchased in 2018, part number 50)

- ▶ washing uniform parts/taking uniforms to the dry cleaners
- ▶ verifying your instrument inventory
- ▶ updating repair records
- ▶ reorganizing the music library (making sure all pieces are in score order with no missing parts)
- ▶ planning music activities for ensemble members to attend (concerts by other schools, musical productions, professional band or orchestra concerts, etc.)
- ▶ coaching after-school ensembles such as flags, winter guard, flute choir, Dixieland combo, etc. (These will require volunteers with experience in the areas of instruction.)
- ▶ updating bulletin boards

Summer is a great time to address these often-overlooked responsibilities and necessities. By planning ahead, you're certain to be prepared for the coming year(s)! ■

Compelling Questions that Encourage Higher-Order Thinking

As educational reform sweeps the country and we're asked to teach in ways that may be new or different, the kinds of questions we use to encourage student learning evolve. Below are some examples of questions we can ask our students to foster deep learning in the music ensemble classroom.

Easy questions begin with: *What . . ., Why . . ., How . . ., When . . ., Who . . .* etc. Answers to these kinds of questions are often short, regurgitated facts that have been learned or memorized. These are questions requiring very little comparative knowledge but are important in early stages of learning. We might ask questions such as: Who wrote this piece? What other piece is in our folders by the same composer? What is the dynamic marking at letter G?

More rigorous questions often include: *Compare . . ., Interpret . . ., Support . . ., Explain . . ., Summarize . . ., Rephrase . . ., and Classify . . . .* These terms require students to think about more than one answer, combining information to create a more knowledgeable response. We ask these questions when we are discussing why there are different dynamics or where it is appropriate to breathe. Answers are often in two parts: "The composer wants us to change dynamics here, otherwise the repeat would sound exactly the same as the first time through." Or perhaps the answers to our questions require explanation: "The repeat of the trio in this march is just like most marches. The first time through is quite soft, often with some parts left out, then the repeat is at a louder level and includes all the written parts."

Problem solving requires applying previous knowledge to situations like: *What would happen if . . ., Which of these facts show . . ., What questions would you ask if . . ., How would you apply what you learned to . . ., Demonstrate your understanding of . . ., Using what you've learned, how (why or what) . . ., What is the relationship between . . .,* and similar questions such as, "*Listening to the recording of what we just played demonstrates what?*" "*How can we improve this section's intonation?*" "*What do we need to do to balance these chords?*"

As we ask our students questions that require higher-level thinking skills, consider incorporating the following into your rehearsals:

▶ How can you change this to make it better?

▶ Can you predict what will happen when . . .

- ▶ What facts support your opinion?
    - ▶ What can you do to minimize . . .
    - ▶ What can you do to maximize . . .
    - ▶ Is there an alternative you believe will work?
    - ▶ Why do you think Bach wrote it this way?
    - ▶ How should we phrase this line and what makes you think so?
    - ▶ What are our options?
    - ▶ How is this staccato style different from the one in the march and why does the same symbol mean so many different things?
    - ▶ What are the stylistic changes we can make so this sounds more like a chorale?
    - ▶ If you were the composer what would you want to have happen here?

Performing music entails endless split-second decisions, but the decisions students make must be grounded in understanding of stylistic considerations, intonation problems, phrasing, articulation, and rhythmic consistency. Higher-level questioning helps students become more knowledgeable and better able to discuss, evaluate, analyze, and create music. Applying their understanding to their performances allows them to fully participate in the process of music making while relating to music on a more academic level. Our challenge as music educators is to be sure the academic emphasis doesn't replace the aesthetic part of making music. ■

Quick Tips and Considerations

Cell phone solutions

In schools where cell phones are allowed, here's a way to be sure they're not being used in your classroom:

Purchase several power strips and plug them in around the perimeter of your classroom. Allow students to charge their phones during rehearsal. This keeps the phones off music stands where you can't see them and allows students to concentrate on what you're teaching. Be sure to remind students daily to silence the ringer. If your principal will support you, dock students a letter grade if they are caught using their phone during class. This will show students that you are serious about cell phone use. The flip side of this is that you must show them that you believe that the rehearsal time is valuable by not wasting time during class and by being ready for class to start each day. This shows them that what goes on in your class is important.

Another option: Hang an old cassette tape storage unit in the front of your classroom and ask students to place their phones there until after class. This keeps phones a good distance from potential users. Anyone whose phone rings during class is docked a letter grade, not for the day, but at the end of the grading period. Again, students will know you're serious.

Starting on time

Do you have students who rush to leave your class because their next teacher locks the door or docks their grade or assigns extra work if they are late? Are you concerned because, though they hurry on at the end of class, they wander in late to yours? Observing other teachers will often give you clues to solving concerns that you are experiencing, so consider talking with colleagues about their solutions or, better yet, observe the first few minutes of their classes. Realize that you will minimize problems if you're ready to begin class on time every day and you expect students to be ready as well. Consider developing a daily warmup routine that begins as soon as you turn on an amplified metronome. This gives an audible cue that class has begun. Turn on the metronome at exactly the same time every day so students know what to expect, but be sure to allow ample though not excessive time for them to assemble instruments and get to their seats. Think about a small penalty you can impose on folks who aren't ready in time, to encourage them to strive for readiness. As you develop this new routine, be sure to praise them on days when everyone is ready on time.

Making music in a room full of strangers

It's hard for students to take the musical risks necessary to prepare outstanding performances. It's even harder to do it in a room full of people they barely know. Solos and other exposed parts are downright scary when students feel they are being judged by their peers. Take away this stigma by having everyone learn the names of the people around them and, eventually, everyone in the class. There are several ways to accomplish this: weekly quizzes with ten to twelve names, daily identification during swabbing at the end of the class, have several students stand each day and introduce themselves, etc. The method is not as important as the results. This is especially important for students with unusual or difficult-to-pronounce names. Everyone deserves to be known by the correct name. And, it's much easier and more enjoyable to make music in a room full of friends.

Planning for winter: The Farmer's Almanac

For those living in areas where snow days can cause excess stress during preparation for Assessment (or any performance) check *The Farmer's Almanac* for the predicted snowfall prior to selecting your music for adjudication. A quick look at the weather predictions for the months of your preparation can help you decide whether to push your group to learn music at a more advanced level or not, depending on anticipated bad weather. If you are waffling between taking your group at a "difficult 4" or an "easy 5," considering the weather forecasts can make a huge difference in how relaxed you and your ensemble feel when time for judging comes. At the very least, it will allow you to enjoy the snow days as much as the students will. People who are in the habit of checking have found that it is more accurate than they expect.

Sight reading: "1-2-3, tempo, time, and key"

Do your students frequently start pieces without checking the key signature, requiring you to then stop rehearsal to fix missed accidentals? Try this (or any) mnemonic device. Before starting a piece of music, say "1-2-3 . . ." and wait for students to reply "tempo, time, and key." The idea is that they will look at each item on their music as they say it. If they reach out and touch these places on their music (the tempo indicator, the time signature, and the key signature), they will remember even better as more senses are in play. This works well for all students but especially for younger ones. Eventually, you can just hold up the fingers and they will think the reply while checking their parts.

Solving budget problems with program fees

Having enough money in your budget to do all the things necessary to run an excellent program is becoming a pipe dream in today's world. Aside from doing fundraisers all year long, consider this option for raising repair monies: Ask each student who borrows a school instrument to pay an instrument use fee. This could be $20–30 per instrument for the year. It is much less expensive than rental programs (though this does not replace the need for rental programs; this is for borrowing school instruments for the year).

If parents complain, explain that the fee is only to help defray the cost of cleaning the instrument after your child is done with it and before it gets handed to the next child. Explain that to borrow a trombone for four years at $25 means that they have invested $100 (rather than the rental fees for four years) and that the chemical cleaning and disinfecting of that instrument (which, by the way, was also done before their child got the instrument) is about $80, leaving $20 for miscellaneous repairs during the years. Water key corks, stuck slides, dings, and dents will certainly cost more, so they're really getting quite a deal.

If they get an instrument at home, the same fee applies. For strings, the monies collected will barely pay for new strings every two to three years, but it's a help. Be sure to clear this with the administration. First, find out whether there is a precedent. Do other classes or activities such as physical education or art club require a fee for consumables? Consider also offering that students who receive free or reduced meals may have the fee waived or a $5/week arrangement to pay it off.

Spare reeds

It seems that no matter how much you remind, demand, and cajole, there is always someone who doesn't have a working reed. Either the last one just broke ("Where are the other two you're always supposed to have in rotation?") or getting to a music store is an impossibility ("My mom says we'll go this weekend because we haven't been able to go this year") or all the rest of the ones in the box are the "rejects" that squeak or don't play well in some octave. Sometimes it's just a matter of kids who can't afford reeds or whose parents aren't supportive. Consider asking students who advance to the next reed strength to donate their unused softer reeds to your program. Elementary teachers can talk to their middle school colleagues about a reed hand-me-down program; middle school teachers enlist their high school colleagues. Most of the time, those softer reeds just get shoved to the bottom of the case or the back of the locker anyway. This way they get put to good use.

Gender identification

Educators must be sensitive to the fact that many students don't always identify with either "girl" or "boy." When you address your ensembles, consider using all-inclusive terms like "Could everyone please take their seats?" or "Folks, it's time to get started." Using limiting terms like "ladies and gentlemen" or excluding terms like "hey guys" can be offensive to students who are already struggling with their identity. While "All y'all" may work in some parts of the United States, find an inclusive term that works for you (friends, family, everyone, musicians, scholars, folks, etc.) and use it. You may never hear how appreciated you are, but there will likely be students in your class who feel more comfortable as a result of your effort.

Using mindful warmups to teach performance skills

It is important that the skills utilized during all aspects of rehearsal, but specifically the warmup, teach and reinforce performance skills. Warmups provide a chance to recall the good results of the previous rehearsal and prepare to move forward and improve.

- ▶ **Long tones.** Don't let this part of the warmup become routine. Focus on producing the best possible sound that is in tune and balanced with the rest of the ensemble.

- ▶ **Rhythms.** Teach a specific routine for counting that is used every time. Whether it is "one-and-two-ee-and" or "ta-ta-ti-ti-ta" doesn't matter, as long as it is always the same. Encourage students to count aloud as they clap. Reinforcing rhythm should be part of the daily warmup.

- ▶ **Buzzing.** Include lip slurs, both down and up, as well as articulated notes. Encourage students to match pitch with their buzz. If they can buzz it, they can play it!

- ▶ **Watching.** Be sure to include some chorales with fermata and phrases so students get in the habit of watching, releasing together, and re-entering together. Focus also on balance and good intonation.

- ▶ **Articulation.** Include various forms of articulation, perhaps with scales or rhythmic exercises, to reinforce consistency of articulation styles across the ensemble. Be aware that using a "tizzle" puts the tongue high in the oral cavity and tends to add extreme air pressure at a level which most instruments never use. This is counterproductive to good tone quality and should be avoided.

When you or the students stop participating fully in the warmup, it becomes a static repetition of fundamentals rather than a set of exercises that are critical to the success of each rehearsal. Be sure that full, concentrated effort is given to each aspect of the warmup and expect the absolute best each day. Setting the standard during the warmup encourages full participation throughout the rest of the rehearsal. Music is always active, never passive or routine!

The Scatter Rehearsal

This is a wonderful rehearsal technique to try about 2-weeks before a performance. Have students sit anywhere in the room that they choose. The only rule – they must not sit next to someone who plays the same part that they do. Encourage folks who normally sit toward the front to sit toward the back and vice-versa. (Be prepared for the snare player who sets up the snare right next to you!)

Play through your performance pieces and encourage students to adjust for balance and intonation with those who now sit around them. Melody parts that were once in the front of the ensemble and easily heard may need to project more strongly from the back and accompaniment parts now being played in the front row may need to be much softer.

At the end of rehearsal ask questions like these: Did anyone struggle with keeping up with their part now that the parts around you are different? What did you do to fix that? What parts did you hear that you've never heard before? Were they melody or harmony? Did anyone have to adjust their volume to be able to hear the melody?

Doing this allows students to awaken their listening skills, learning to adjust to new sounds around them. It also points out parts they may have never heard before, making them more aware of what the music involves.

If space allows, having a rehearsal in a large circle (with the conductor in the middle) is also an ear-opening experience for all. The bottom line is this - adding variety and increased awareness to your rehearsals and performance can bring several positive results! ■

There's No Excuse . . . .

There's no excuse . . .

. . . for being late. You're a professional and time is contractual.

. . . for yelling at an individual student/colleague. Talking gets the same message across at a lower volume.

. . . for blaming the entire class for the actions of a few. Some in the class will take it very personally, even though it may not have been directed at them in the first place. Isolate the few and speak directly with them.

. . . FOR SENDING E-MAILS THAT SEEM LIKE YOU'RE YELLING ALL THE TIME

. . . for swearing in front of the students or subordinates. There are many other word choices, and demonstrating your quality education will get better results than stooping to the gutter.

. . . for swearing at a parent. Even if they start it! You're the professional. Act like one at all times.

. . . for speaking to students in their street language. An educated adult demonstrating proper language skills helps students learn to succeed in the world outside their neighborhood. You don't need to sound snobby, just well-spoken.

. . . for posting anything on social media about students, parents, peers, the administration, your boss, the superintendent, etc. If you have a negative or frustrating experience, vent to close friends or colleagues. Or keep your bad day to yourself. Wait twenty-four hours before acting.

. . . for not having grades done on time. Deadlines are known well in advance and, again, it's contractual.

. . . not planning well for each day. "I'm not getting paid to work at night" may be true, but then you need to find time during the day to plan the next day's work. "Winging it" is never a good path to success.

. . . for grousing about your job. If you're not happy, start looking for something else to do. Recertify, change schools/companies, or start a social group that meets weekly to hang out and vent, maybe over food.

. . . for having a bad day. They are self-perpetuating. If you wake up grumpy, treat yourself to something different for breakfast so your mood will improve. Take muffins to your colleagues. Or doughnut holes. Buy a box of coffee to share. By contributing to everyone else's morning, you'll likely improve yours.

. . . for not dressing appropriately for work. Even if you feel like "death," make the effort. It will improve your day as well as the experiences of those with whom you come into contact. Blue jeans, pajama pants, and sweats are not appropriate for teachers! Khakis, twills, denim skirts—there are lots of other comfortable, more professional options.

. . . for not taking a "mental health day" when you feel you really need a break. As long as you don't waste your sick days, you'll have the ability to take a day now and then to regroup, refresh, and recharge. But don't abuse the opportunity.

. . . for not asking for help with a sticky problem that is bothering you. Ask colleagues, supervisors, maybe even the boss. There are always more experienced folks available to help you brainstorm.

. . . for staying in a job that causes you constant stress. Remember: You don't owe anybody anything that is more important than what you owe yourself. If your job is literally making you sick, it's time to redirect your life. Maybe transferring to a different school, office, or city is all you need.

. . . for not doing your very best every single day. Be prepared and be enthusiastic! Be passionate about what you do. You will get back what you give, so give your all! ■

"Wah-wah, wah wah wah-wah wah!": On Talking Less and Being Heard

Like the droning, unintelligible adult voices in *Peanuts* animated features, it is easy for music teachers to talk so much in rehearsals that students hardly hear them anymore. Reminders about key and time signatures, explanations of stylistic demands, accidentals, fingerings, consistency, energy, how to perform a passage even more smoothly, how to articulate, vocal enunciation, rhythmic pulsing, the composer's intent, the backstory of the piece being rehearsed, tempos, announcements of upcoming concerts and fundraisers—directors of successful programs can easily spend a quarter of the rehearsal talking.

Since everything we discuss in rehearsal is extremely important, how do we get the students to stay tuned in to what we're saying?

One theory is this: students signed up for band (or orchestra or choir) to perform music! The more they can play or sing, the more they'll enjoy the class. Yet directors must explain so many elements while preparing pieces for performance. Try this: When you stop, say what you need to communicate in ten words or fewer. Even if this means stopping more frequently at first, students begin to anticipate the fact that they will start playing or singing again very soon.

Having watched rehearsals where the directors' talking has taken up well over half of the allotted time, this seems like a good option. Obviously, well-constructed, grammatically correct sentences cannot be used when speaking economically. Use brief comments like "Consistent articulations needed—slight separation of accented notes," "Play much softer, but keep air intense," "Clarinets, check pitch on that," or "Lovely. Repeat exactly the same but more *legato*." Each of these comments follow something in the music that isn't as polished as it should be. Stopping, identifying the problem/solution, and repeating the passage all takes place in a very short amount of time. Students barely have time to put their instruments down before it's time to play again. Even that small act will add minutes to your rehearsals.

If this seems impossible, consider ten-word responses except for once or twice per class period to help you ease into the stricter model. Then reduce that over the next few weeks to be just ten words. Once you've mastered that, try for five- to seven-word responses. There are teachers who can restrict themselves to three words with some level of success.

Another option is the silent rehearsal. This needs a bit of setup the day before. Explain that no words will be used, only gestures. Post the title of the piece(s) to be rehearsed. Conduct the regular warmup (so no talking is needed), tune, then point to the title or hold up the score. It is the director's job, during the rehearsal, to stop as needed and show, via body language and baton technique, what needs to be changed. Write rehearsal numbers on the board, if needed. Conducting is a form of nonverbal communication. Let conducting communicate what you want from the music.

If you think you're not talking much at all, put your theory to the test. Ask a colleague or reliable student to sit with a stop watch, turning it on each time you stop the ensemble to speak. The stop watch is turned off again once the group begins to play. At the end of rehearsal, see how much time was spent talking, explaining, admonishing, encouraging, informing, and reinforcing. If it's more than 10% of your rehearsal, consider trying the "ten words" approach.

If nothing else, these exercises will help you realize how much time you spend talking. Rather than praising every little accomplishment, save the praise for the end of the rehearsal, while students swab out and pack up. Compliments, given once, are taken seriously. Compliments given repeatedly throughout rehearsal, while meant to encourage, often become an ignored drone that eats up time that could be spent making music. A nod of the head, a smile, or a thumbs-up will suffice most of the time. And please don't get into the habit of saying, "Good!" when it's not!

Good luck! Minimizing speaking can make a huge difference in what can be accomplished in rehearsal, and your students may enjoy class much more.

Note: Sometimes in a particularly intense or lengthy rehearsal, it is necessary to give players, especially brass, some time with their mouthpieces off their face. This is a great time to talk about larger concepts that can't be communicated in ten words or less. This is okay, when used sparingly and with intention. The problem comes when *all* communication lasts a minute or more. Look around your rehearsals. Are students fidgeting, talking, checking cell phones, greasing slides, looking bored? Let them play for 90% of the class period and see if that changes. And consider, when asking questions for students to answer, holding *them* to the "ten words or fewer" rule. ∎

3

Auditioning

The Criteria: Taking the Anxiety Out of Auditions

Auditions are many students' least favorite thing. One way that directors can make auditioning as stress-free as possible for the students—whether they're auditioning for placement in a particular ensemble, for seating within the ensemble, or for acceptance into a program—is to be clear with the student about how they are being judged.

The audition rubric that follows is a starting point. Hang it up so that students can see and understand the areas in which they will be judged. Young musicians typically think that a good audition is about hitting the correct notes. How many times have you heard, "But I didn't make any mistakes!" or "She made more mistakes than I did!" when consoling a student about their placement. Using a rubric will show them that you are listening to many aspects of their playing, not just correct pitches. If each of the rubric points address techniques that you specifically work on in class, it is a great reinforcement for what you are teaching.

The nine categories in the rubric shown here should give you all the criteria you need if you're holding band auditions. You'll need to make adjustments for string and vocal auditions, but you can see how much easier this can make the whole process.

Here's how it is designed to work: Use one rubric for each person auditioning. During the audition, put checks in the boxes that appropriately reflect what you're hearing. If more than one excerpt is being used, consider using little numbers—1 for the first excerpt, 2 for the second, etc. At the end, glance at the sheet and make an overall judgement of the musical status of the student. There is space at the top for the student's name and instrument, and space at the bottom for comments.

While listening to each musician, make decisions about part and seat placement and jot them down; your first impression is probably accurate.

The rubric helps students understand what is important in the audition, and it gives you the chance to specifically consider where each student's strengths and weaknesses lie. It also allows you to show them areas for improvement. Just remember: If you're going to share the results with the students, be sure that all comments and notes you write are constructive. Even when identifying areas for improvement, keep it positive. This will be far more beneficial for you *and* the students both in the short run and the long run. ■

Name:

Instrument:

POSTURE is poor. Instrument is not being supported.	**POSTURE** is fair but not what it should be.	**POSTURE** is good. Effort is being made to use correct playing position.	**POSTURE** is excellent.
BREATHING is shallow and unsupported.	**BREATHING** has little regard for the music.	**BREATHING** utilizes full support and phrasing	**BREATHING** is full and occurs in appropriate places for musical phrasing.
TONE is uneven and weak. Lacks proper breath support.	**TONE** is thin and not characteristic of the instrument. Lacks resonance.	**TONE** is supported and shows characteristic qualities.	**TONE** is full, supported, and a model of warm, characteristic sound.
VIBRATO is not present at all.	**VIBRATO** is not present or is very shaky and unregulated.	**VIBRATO** is beginning to have a role in the sound. It is used well.	**VIBRATO** is used appropriately and enhances the overall tone quality.
RHYTHM is uneven or incorrect at times. Rhythmic relationships are not exact.	**RHYTHM** lacks precision. Some notes/rests are too short or too long. Values aren't correct.	**RHYTHM** is mostly accurate and in tempo. Effort made to maintain steady tempo.	**RHYTHM** is precise, accurate, and well-executed. Tempo is steady.
DYNAMICS are not as indicated in the music.	**DYNAMICS** don't apply all the time or aren't appropriate.	**DYNAMICS** are effective most of the time. Effort made at providing contrast.	**DYNAMICS** are conveyed successfully. Good contrast between the markings. Consistent use enhances the music.
ARTICULATIONS are random; not as indicated.	**ARTICULATIONS** are inconsistent or often lacking.	**ARTICULATIONS** are present and usually accurate.	**ARTICULATIONS** are accurate, consistent, and appropriate for the style of the music.
STYLE of the music lacks consistency and is not communicated well.	**STYLE** is not expressed correctly for the pieces played.	**STYLE** is evident in the performance. Contrasts exist between pieces.	**STYLE** is always appropriate and well communicated.
SCALES have many incorrect notes or require several attempts. Or not all scales are performed ____ ____ 1 octave 2 octaves	**SCALES** are not smooth or rhythmic. Several incorrect notes. ____ ____ 1 octave 2 octaves	**SCALES** are well-played and mostly accurate. Attempt at memorizing is somewhat successful. ____ ____ 1 octave 2 octaves	**SCALES** are memorized, and/or performed fluidly and with very few errors. ____ ____ 1 octave 2 octaves

Comments:

The Process: Ensuring that Students Understand What Auditions Show

Why do we bother to audition everyone year after year? We know how they play. We know who works at it and who doesn't. Why not just put them in a group or seat based on what we know? It saves so much time and hassle.

Yet students can surprise us. When given the opportunity to improve their ensemble or their seat, many students will go the extra distance to be sure they achieve that next level. By placing folks based on our impressions, we forfeit their right to try to better themselves. The little bit of competition that is created by auditions can inspire students to excel. Some will take the bait. Others may not. But those are things that help shape the expectations that we, the directors, have for the group.

One director used a major scale sheet as the "I care" test. Students knew they would be asked to play the entire set of twelve major scales as part of their audition for next year's bands. Most prepared at least moderately successfully. Some played only the more familiar scales, skipping over or struggling through the more difficult keys. But then there were the ones who whipped right through all the scales, often memorized and in multiple octaves. They became the leaders. They were the ones who passed the "I care" test with flying colors. By not holding auditions, how can those who are singularly motivated show their dedication? Some were shy, quiet souls who surprised others with their achievements. Others were found at the ends of sections, just waiting for their turn to surprise. And, yes, some were the expected ones. But not all!

Auditioning students is time-consuming. Consider doing it in stages. The scale sheet can be done in one week during class sometime in the year. Minor scales and chromatic scales can be tested during another week. Neither takes a whole class period if ten to twelve students are heard each day. Or consider having your students record scales or send them to you via computer. That only leaves the actual audition pieces, and maybe sight reading, which can be done during class or after school with multiple auditions taking place each day. Students who are finished can work quietly in their seats. Students waiting to audition can finger through their music. Students not auditioning that day often look up when they hear something impressive, and the recognition that some players are stronger than others takes place right in the classroom. Because students may be auditioning in front of their peers, many practice more than they otherwise might. It's a winning situation all around.

Some teachers are fortunate enough to have all their trumpets, or clarinets, or flutes, etc. studying with the same private teacher. In this case, it is respectful to have a conversation with the teacher before assigning seats. Having their input is often enlightening and will make for a stronger section.

Explaining ensemble seating helps eliminate disputes and hard feelings. Having students recognize the importance of good players on second and third parts rather than all the strongest players on first part is critical to their understanding that a balanced ensemble is the final goal. Sometimes keeping a strong player in the second band as principal provides better experiences than putting them last chair in a more advanced group. There are certainly more chances for solos. These concepts are difficult for students to grasp because most students want a higher seat in a higher band. However, increased knowledge is the key to reducing the strife and hurt feelings that can result from auditions. Once students realize the reasons behind the seating, they are more likely to accept their assigned place without question. ▪

4

Traveling with Your Ensemble

Domestic Travel Hints and Helps

Deciding to travel

Traveling with your ensemble(s) can be a wonderful addition to your program as it offers the chance to perform in other venues, work at team building within the group, and possibly have your group(s) evaluated by directors and professionals outside your locale. However, it is very time-consuming and expensive, so ask yourself these questions before you make the decision to travel:

▶ Do I trust the members of the ensemble to represent the school in a totally positive way both musically and with their behavior?

▶ Do I believe the parents will support the idea of travel?

▶ Can they afford it?

▶ Can I plan enough fundraisers to allow students who need financial help to participate?

▶ Can I get 90% or more of the group to commit to participating?

▶ Is there anything on the school calendar that conflicts with the dates I'm proposing?

▶ Is the trip I'm planning a good musical experience?

▶ Is the trip I'm planning a good educational experience?

Before you plan: Points to consider

▶ Taking young people on trips sometimes comes with baggage that you will need to address before you leave. Here's an example: A colleague's small student group from a metropolitan school went to a competition several states away. While there, one of the girls dared another to steal something from a store. After her success, several girls tried to do the same. They were caught and taken to the police station, where an administrator on the trip bailed them out. The parents were called, and transportation was arranged for the girls to be sent home at their parents' expense. The competition was ruined, and the group was not allowed to travel any more.

▶ Parents need to be supportive of the trip before you mention it to the students. Schedule a meeting or send an e-mail. Present the estimated cost of the trip with a list of what is included (lodging, certain meals, the festival, transportation, insurance, admissions to attractions, etc.) and what is extra (any meals the students are responsible for getting themselves), plus an itinerary, including museums and fun activities. Remember to include monies for tips and hotel expenses for bus drivers. If there are meals that the students must get on their own, consider including a meal stipend in the trip estimate and give each student a packet of meal money to use for those meals. Plan for the total to be a bit more than you think it might be, as additional expenses will come up. It's much better to tell parents the last payment will be smaller than expected.

▶ How many students will need financial help? How many parents are willing to donate extra so that others can participate? (*See the commitment form in Step 2 later in this chapter.*) Is there another destination that is less expensive but still offers a great musical and educational experience? Consider offering parents the choice of which event the ensemble(s) will attend.

▶ Do you have the time to organize and run several fundraisers or do you have parents who are willing to head each of them? Are the fundraisers the sort that will bring good money? Selling candy is great but for a fifty-cent profit for each bar, kids have to sell 200 bars to earn $100. Are the parents who need financial help willing to organize one of the fundraisers?

▶ Fundraising so that all can attend is critical. If the point of the trip is the music festival or performance, going with less than the entire group means the "team" is divided. There may always be one or two who can't participate because of prior commitments, but always strive to take the entire group.

▶ Standardized testing and AP exams are often only available once. Make sure you're not leaving students out because of something else they're committed to. (*Note*: Many years ago, a student took an AP test in Bermuda while on an orchestra trip. AP tests are often given on the same day everywhere!)

- First and foremost, plan a worthwhile musical event. If you're using a festival company, is the festival promoting the things you feel are important to the development of your program? Are you looking for a competitive festival or one that will offer comments only? Some offer on-stage clinics with your ensemble as the springboard to demonstrate ideas, while others have off-stage clinics where someone talks with your group and answers questions. Some are built around attending an amusement park; others offer cultural activities. Some just act as travel agents. Choose a company that has a great track record and check references. If you are booking the entire trip yourself to save money, recognize that this means much more of your time and perhaps not much savings. Some festival companies get special rates for hotels and admission tickets because they book and buy in bulk.

- Including educational experiences is a great way to win the approval of your administration. Visiting a science museum and historical sites added to attending a concert, musical, or special rehearsal means that the students have a well-balanced experience. If the festival is associated with an amusement park, be sure your school system allows this, as some don't. While it's recommended that you plan something fun for your students, be sure to keep the focus on education and especially on the musical aspect.

Moving forward

Step 1. Put together a realistic cost estimate. Make a list of exactly what is included (meals, lodging, the festival, transportation, travel trailer for instruments, insurance, admissions to attractions and sightseeing, tips for the bus drivers and tour guides, etc.) and what is *not* included (any meals students must get on their own, souvenirs, etc.). Including the cost of everything is an easy way to ensure that all students have everything they need for the entire trip, even if it means organizing and paying for extra meals in advance or giving students a packet of cash to pay for meals not already included. Having collected all the monies and then telling parents to send their children with $100 for meals and incidentals creates an awkward situation if parents aren't expecting this.

Step 2. Present your plan to the parents. This can be done at a pre-trip meeting or via e-mail, but parents need to be on board before the students know of the possibility of a trip. Right from the start, let parents know that the goal of the trip is musical and that you are expecting that the entire ensemble will participate. Ask parents for a "yes or no" vote, perhaps like the one below:

_____ Yes! I want my child to participate!

_____ I want my child to participate but I will need help raising funds for the trip.

_____ My child can participate and I can make a donation toward helping another student.

_____ My child will be unable to participate.

_____ I would like to go as a chaperone.

Student name: _____

Parent name:_____

It is important that parents understand that, in addition to the musical aspect of the trip, you have planned interesting educational activities and fun ones as well.

Step 3. Tally the responses. Determine whether there are enough acceptances to make the trip work. Here's where logic needs to step in. If fewer than 90% of your group can participate, it's not really a band trip. Consider calling parents you feel may be borderline in their decision or who declined only because of finances. Take a look at how many are willing to make donations. If you gave "scholarships," would some of the hesitant parents change their mind? How much do you need for scholarships? Are the parents who need financial help willing to do fundraising? Do you have several fundraising projects in mind? Once you determine that the trip is a possibility, line up parents who need financial help to chair the fundraisers. If there are still fewer than 90% on board, seriously consider postponing the trip until the next year, when parents would have time to put aside money for the trip. Although the oldest students will have moved on, it is more important to have as close to 100% participation as possible. Otherwise your team is divided and will suffer consequences to the *esprit de corps*. A good rule of thumb is that no one gets left behind because of financial difficulty. There are ways to earn!

Step 4. If you've decided to postpone, let the parents know. Be honest. If you're postponing because of finances, ask parents to set aside a little each month between now and next fall. Tell them the first payment will be half the total and give them an exact date that it will be due. Because the students were never told or involved, there is no friction in class. If you've decided to proceed, start by getting the students excited about fundraising. Set a payment schedule, with the first payment of one half as the deposit. The deposit indicates to you, with certainty, who is participating. You can still communicate with parents of students who are not signing on to see if you can convince them. Stress the importance of the entire musical ensemble being together.

Note: It is critical that participation in a national level music festival includes at least 90% of your ensemble. Fewer than that and you run the risk of an inferior performance that will have negative effects on your program. (*See "Exchange Concerts" below for a less expensive option.*)

Step 5. Assuming that you're moving ahead, start the paperwork required by your school system. Be sure the school principal is on board with your plans. A well-balanced, educational, and fun trip might include the following:

- ▶ the music festival performance
- ▶ a visit to area science or history museum or historical sites
- ▶ a visit to an art museum
- ▶ attendance at a concert or musical near your destination or *en route*
- ▶ attendance at a rehearsal of a professional band or orchestra in the area
- ▶ a day at an amusement park or hands-on discovery museum
- ▶ a hop-aboard guided bus tour of the town, pointing out interesting or historical sights
- ▶ a visit to and walking tour of a college campus

If you are travelling during spring break, have you made arrangements for students to attend religious services while away? If traveling over a weekend, can time for church or temple be fit into your plans?

Step 6. If you're working with a festival company, let your representative know your maximum budget per child. Ask that they arrange for breakfast buffet and dinner every night. Starting the day with a hearty meal will guarantee that everyone is fully awake and engaged in the day's activities. Lunch money could be part of a packet of cash handed to each student, as lunch is the easiest meal to get separately. Whenever possible, have meals together.

A trip where the focus drifts away from the musical performance means that you're becoming a travel agent rather than a music teacher.

Fundraising

Choosing fundraisers that earn quick money means fewer programs are needed. Wreaths, baked goods, and fruit are good because they get used up quickly and can be repeated month to month or year to year, and the profit margins can be $3–10 per item. Candles and wrapping paper are generally successful only once. Consider trading work (leaf raking, lawn mowing, snow shoveling, car washing) for cash, as it is all profit. Car washes done for "donations" often bring more money than charging a set fee per car. Rent-a-team programs are great for getting yards raked because students go in groups for safety and the job is finished sooner. Ask the homeowner to provide leaf bags.

Selling advertising space in program booklets are a great way to raise almost pure profit. Ask businesses, private teachers, realtors, and parents who own or operate small businesses or services like editing or printing, to "buy" advertising space in a program that will be handed out at a couple of concerts. Ask the printing shop to donate the cost of printing in exchange for an ad, and everything is profit. It's possible for a student to pay for a whole trip by selling a few full-page ads. Check with your yearbook advisor to see how much ads sell for. If you hand out the brochures at more than one concert you can charge more for your ad, as multiple views is a more attractive option for the advertisers. Consider $250 for a full page, $500 for the centerfold, $125 for a half page, $75 for a quarter, $40 for an eighth of a page (slightly smaller than a business card). Parents can also buy ad space to wish their child well. Grandparents are often willing to do the same.

There are two ways to approach fundraising: 1) Everyone participates and the monies earned go toward reducing the cost for everyone, or 2)

People who need financial help participate and the profit they earn goes toward the cost of their trip. The second method encourages those who need money most to work hardest and reduces the number of complaints that "so-and-so isn't doing their share" when all are working together toward a shared goal. In some cases, those who don't need financial help may donate their fundraising profits to those who do.

Consider asking companies and elected officials for donations. PTAs sometimes can make a donation toward an educational trip, as can local businesses. Ask local businesses to pick up the cost of printing concert programs during the year so you can put what you would have spent toward the scholarship fund. Put their ad in the concert program and be sure to thank them.

Collecting money

Consider collecting payments in halves or thirds, with the final payment due two months before you travel.

Line up parents or a parent committee to come to school on the days that payments are due. Make three-part receipts for each payment—one to the student, two for you. (More on this below.) Keep a spreadsheet that includes deposits and fundraising profits for each student (to be subtracted from the last two payments), and post it periodically so students can check what they've contributed. Ask parents who can to make donations to help others come up with enough money. Distribute the extra cash as scholarships that go directly into the trip accounts.

After two thirds of the payment and most of the fundraising has been done, have a parent volunteer prepare account sheets for each family. List fundraising profits earned for each fundraiser and attach one of the remaining receipts for each of the payments made. This lets families know exactly what they have earned and paid, and is a great chance to be sure you've included everything. They will let you know if you missed something!

Lessons from a festival adjudicator

So many times, groups with inferior or barely average performances are missing large parts of their ensemble. The team is broken. It's not helpful for building your program if the group's performance is anything less than the best it can be. Identifying some students as "the trip band" is dividing your group into the "haves" and the "have nots" and can create friction within the ensemble.

Pulling a small group out of your large ensemble to perform as a separate ensemble only works if the pull-out group has adequate time to rehearse and perfect their performance. When groups share performers in order to participate in more categories, the effort often backfires, as the "select" group doesn't perform as well. The goal shouldn't be to compete in as many categories as possible, but rather to bring the very best performances to the festival.

Be aware of how many performances you ask your students to play in one day. Playing in the big concert band, the select wind ensemble, and the jazz band is a lot of playing in a short time period, and the last ensemble's performance quality is likely to suffer.

A word about being part of the audience: A critically important part of the experience is to hear other groups perform. Be sure to be a polite audience for your own groups as well as those from other schools. Applaud, but don't cheer or whistle—a concert is not a sporting event.

Lessons from a seasoned band traveler

Don't allow students to wear blue jeans, sweat pants, or pajama pants. Khakis, black jeans, pink, green, white, or purple jeans are fine, but blue jeans, sweats, and pajama pants create a very relaxed and casual attitude, often keeping students from always being on their best behavior. You will find that your students are treated better than other student groups because they look nicer. The director needs to dress so as to be easily identified as the adult in charge. A tie is a must for men, except at the amusement park.

Let students know right from the beginning that you expect them to behave properly and that they are governed by school system rules even though they are away from school. Be specific about no drinking or smoking and no drugs. If you feel it is warranted, plan a "search and seizure" in the parking lot before the bus leaves. Be sure the student is standing by their luggage when this is done and that two chaperones are involved. Women go through girls' suitcases and carry-ons; men chaperones search the boys. It is best if the ensemble director stands by as a witness rather than performing searches. This may seem harsh but a trip with no problems will do wonders for your program and for your standing in the school.

Consider telling students that at curfew, monitoring tape will be used to secure them in their rooms. (Take a couple of rolls of two-inch-wide masking tape. One three-inch piece is sufficient for each door.) If the tape is unstuck in the morning, the students in the room—all of them—will be sent home with one of the chaperones at their parent's expense. This allows everyone—students, chaperones, the director, and hotel staff—to get a good night's sleep. Chaperone duties include taping the rooms shut at curfew and untaping them at wake-up call. Parents will like knowing that their children will not have the opportunity to sneak out at night, visiting other rooms or, worse, leaving the hotel to wander about. Parents will hopefully make it clear to their students that following the rules is a must. Opening the door with a 3-inch piece of tape is no problem if there is an emergency in the hotel but resealing cannot be done. Students have their chaperone's cell phone number if there is a problem.

Some directors have students "earn" the right to travel by accumulating points during the part of the year leading up to the trip. Points can be earned by completing performance quizzes and written assignments, being on time and prepared for class, good behavior, and just about anything else you can think of. If your point is to eliminate one or two troublemakers from the trip, this will obviously help. Be careful that it doesn't backfire, leaving home the soloist for one of your competition pieces. Consider asking the parent(s) of problem students to chaperone. Assigning those students to a staff member or the administrator chaperone on the trip often works well, too.

If you've got a day planned where students will be on their own for a portion of the day or are planning to spend a day at an amusement park, consider having a local business or music store donate money for matching, brightly colored tee shirts in return for their name being somewhere on the shirt. This helps the chaperones identify your students quickly and helps your students locate each other easily as they go from ride to ride. Any place there is a crowd, matching shirts are a must! Also, students must always explore in groups of two or more.

Exchange concerts

A less expensive option than the festival is the exchange concert. Finding a school in another location that is willing to participate is the first step. Go online and find names of schools in the area you wish to visit. Contact directors until you find one who is interested. Be sure to mention what activities are available in your area—parks, museums, theaters, etc.—that might attract students the same age as yours.

The idea behind an exchange is that group A travels to visit group B. Students from group A are housed with ensemble members and other students from the group B school. A concert is performed featuring both groups. A few weeks later, group B travels to stay with group A. Another concert is performed with both groups contributing alone and perhaps together. Consider preparing the same piece and performing it together at each school with the director at that school conducting.

When accepting volunteers to house visiting students be sure to choose carefully, and ask the other director to do the same. The goal is to ensure that everyone is in a safe and secure environment.

Plan fun and educational activities while the group is visiting your students. The visiting director will then do the same for you and your ensemble.

Advantages of exchange concerts include greatly reduced expenses, much less planning (because it is shared), a noncompetitive musical experience, getting to play your concert pieces twice, and meeting lots of new people. Consider housing students in pairs, as a minimum, so that no one is alone in a different setting.

Disadvantages of exchange concerts include the fact that some students are not comfortable staying in the home of someone they don't know. There is also no adjudication.

The many advantages often outweigh the few problems you may encounter. Several international music festivals include home-stay as the housing option, and many communities are in the habit of hosting visitors. Be sure to have several open conversations with the other host director before deciding that you've found a match.

Chaperone duties

Parent chaperones are necessary for all trips but especially overnight ones. They should understand, in advance, what their responsibilities will be. Here are a few to get you thinking:

▶ Chaperones pay their own way and will be housed in pairs and students are in quads. (You'll need to decide how to pay for the added charge of housing chaperones in pairs rather than quads. Perhaps a percentage of one fundraiser could cover that.)

▶ They will be responsible for _____ students during the trip.

▶ They will tape students in their rooms at curfew and untape them at wakeup call.

▶ Chaperones are expected to be at breakfast to make sure their assigned students are there.

▶ They will keep cell phone numbers of all of their students and contact them (or have students contact chaperones) several times whenever the group is not together. (This works well in theme parks and during free time for shopping or eating.) Check in every two hours.

▶ Chaperones may be responsible for reminding students in their care to take medications.

▶ Chaperones watch their assigned students for signs of illness, homesickness, etc.

▶ If a child is ill and needs to stay in the hotel all day, the assigned chaperone will also stay.

▶ Chaperones will make announcements and reminders as needed at bed check.

▶ Chaperones should be engaged in the daily activities and model expected behaviors.

▶ No drinking or smoking is permitted until after students are in bed for the night.

Whether it's a day trip or an overnight one, be sure parents of participants fill out a medical form listing prescriptions being taken and any over-the-counter meds the students have with them (inhalers, allergy meds, Ibuprofen, epi pens, etc.) plus food allergies. Include parent emergency contact numbers and the doctor's name and phone number in case of emergency. It's often helpful to have copies of the front and back of student medical insurance cards as well. Carry all the forms everywhere the group goes. Medical forms are to be completely confidential!

A few odds and ends

▶ **Emergency cash.** Be sure to take several hundred (a thousand?) dollars in emergency cash. Possible reasons for needing this: taxi to and from the airport if a student needs to rush home for an emergency, taxi to carry anyone with an injury or illness to the doctor, emergency room fees, students who spend their meal money on souvenirs and need a loan.

▶ **Movies for the bus ride.** Be sure the ratings are age-appropriate for everyone in the group.

▶ **Itineraries.** Consider giving everyone a specific itinerary so the group stays on schedule. Include the addresses of sights in case part of the group is separated and must catch up later.

▶ **Water.** Plan to provide water each day if you are at an amusement park or another outside venue.

▶ **Sunscreen.** Remind students to use sunscreen. Burned lips don't buzz!

▶ **Pack light.** Everyone must be able to carry their suitcase and instrument (and backpack or purse?) in one trip. Consider wardrobe boxes from a moving or storage company if you have tuxes and long dresses or skirts. Tape the sides of pant legs and long skirts together so they don't fall off the hanger. Tape coat hangers to the metal bar so hangers won't fall off. These boxes will fit under a coach, lying down. Another option is large suitcases. Tuxes on hangers and folded in half should fit nicely. Dresses fold easily in thirds. Students pack their own shoes, bow ties, etc.

Flying with instruments

Instruments that travel underneath a coach require very little special packing. Care must be taken not to stack heavy instruments on top of smaller ones, and suitcases should not be placed on top of instrument cases. However, when flying, instruments need to be packed differently. Small instruments like flutes, oboes, clarinets, bassoons, violins and violas, trumpets, and some alto saxophones can likely be considered as carry-ons. This is strongly recommended. While the Federal Aviation Administration is supposed to allow all instruments inside the cabin, space restrictions and instrument size often make this impossible. It's better to be prepared.

Plan ahead by packing all instruments to prevent damage. Small woodwinds should be removed from cases and a sheet of small bubble wrap placed in the case. Replace the instrument parts and lay another layer of bubbles over the top before closing. If the case is too small, a single sheet or a sheet of thin, flexible packing foam can be used instead. The goal is to prevent the instrument from moving around inside the case. For trumpets and alto saxophones expected to ride inside the cabin, it's still a good idea to pack the bell with bubble wrap and to put bubble wrap between the valve section and the leadpipe/bell flare. Consider renting travel cases for large instruments from local military bands or music stores. Building crates for large percussion is also an option. Be sure instruments are secure inside the crate.

Strings travelling inside the cabin just need to be secure inside the case—no bouncing around. Perhaps wrap the scroll in a small sheet of foam or small bubbles for extra protection.

Larger woodwinds and brass should be entirely wrapped in bubble wrap and returned to the case. Fill the bell with a bunched-up piece of foam or bubble wrap dense enough to support the metal of the bell. Be sure there is protection at the end of the bell flare as well.

Consider using brightly colored tape to label all suitcase and instrument handles or matching luggage tags so everyone can see what belongs with the group. This is especially important for airline travel when instruments and suitcases have to be taken off the conveyor belt quickly.

Before departing, call to confirm all lodging and meal arrangements and activities made for the group. Be sure you have packed all tickets, vouchers, and confirmation numbers for the trip and have a generous supply of emergency cash.

With careful and complete planning on your part, traveling with your ensemble can be a rewarding and positive experience for everyone. Be sure to choose a destination that everyone can afford so that the entire group can participate. ■

International Travel Hints and Helps

Deciding to take your ensemble outside the boundaries of the United States is a huge commitment of time, energy, and money. However, done well, it can provide once-in-a-lifetime experiences for all who participate. First thing to accept: Your group will probably not reach their highest musical potential in a year when details will take up at least 10% of almost every rehearsal. That said, it is still a terrific experience for all and one worth pursuing.

First, check out the chapter on domestic travel. There is useful information included there that you should consider before proceeding.

Assuming the parents are already behind you on this, and that you have a large percentage (strive for 90% or more!) of students participating, carefully plan your fundraising so that all of the supplemental monies have been raised at least four months prior to travel. Most overseas companies want payment quite early, and it's less expensive if you can buy plane tickets early in the process. The deposit/first payment should be enough to cover the reserve on the air fare. That way, you know who is going so you can order the plane tickets.

Additional items to budget for: fees for checking instruments plus oversize or overweight fees, exchange fees for currency, tips for coach drivers and tour guides, purchasing bottled water for sightseeing days.

Purchase a guide book for the country/countries you'll be visiting. Read it for ideas of what is worth seeing. Share interesting information with the students. Save your receipt for a tax deduction.

Passports

Everyone traveling must have a passport. While it is possible to get one in a couple of weeks, the cost is usually much more, so plan ahead and apply several months before traveling. Have a parent get passport application forms from the post office and pass them out as soon as possible. Find out in advance where passport photos can be taken and provide parents with a list of locations. Also give them a list of locations where passport applications and photos can be turned in. The documents required for first-time passports may take a little time so plan ahead. If anyone's parents are separated or divorced, there are special forms that have to be filed in order for the student to leave the country. If one parent is accompanying the group, there may be forms allowing that parent to leave the country with the child even for married couples. Check the laws in your state so there are no surprises.

As the director, you'll want to have a copy of the photo page of everyone's passport. Set a date for collecting these that is several weeks before departure, just in case you have some procrastinators in the group. Keep a folder with all photo copies (chaperones, too, as well as yours) with you as you travel. If anyone loses their passport or leaves it somewhere that is impossible to get to, you can take the person and their copy to the American embassy and receive permission to leave the country and return to the States.

Vaccinations

Depending on your destination, vaccinations may be required. Check into this well in advance and assign a parent to find out if group discounts can be obtained if they all go to one site.

Insurance

Be sure parents have expensive personal instruments covered by their homeowners insurance. Check your school's policy regarding the school instruments. Health insurance for all travelers can usually be obtained inexpensively from the company that insures the sports teams at your school. Find out if there are limitations (no water sports, no motorcycle riding, no skiing, etc.), and let students and parents know what is not included and will not be permitted on the trip.

Travel agent/trip coordinator

Seriously consider using a travel agent if you are doing a performance tour or a festival company if you are participating in an international music festival. Their connections will provide experiences for your students that you may not be aware of or able to access. Any large American company probably has a representative that books international travel. Call and talk to a few before deciding which one best fits your needs.

Once you've decided, let the trip planner know your maximum budget for each participant. If you have over twenty participants, expect to have one free ticket for each twenty or twenty-five travelers. This often includes only the hotel and festival fees, not air fare, admissions, meals, or taxes. Ask if it includes lodging as well. It's possible to use this savings to defray part of the cost of housing chaperones in double rooms rather than in quads.

It is essential that you read everything that comes from your trip co-ordinator. Many times, important details are buried in the text. Consider reading with a highlighter in your hand to mark things you'll want to recall later in the planning.

Here's a story: A band was going to China with four other bands from their region. Several times in the text, the information stated that performers must bring their own music stands. When everyone was setting up for the massed band rehearsal, only three bands of the five had music stands, and only three bands had brought the needed percussion instruments. The other directors had assumed that music stands, snare drums, bells, and the like would be provided. Because each student in the three bands had brought a stand, there were enough to share for the massed performance. Individual performances, at different sites, were an unexpected challenge.

Chaperones

Be sure you have the minimum number required by your school. If possible, include an administrator and a few staff members in addition to parents. For peace of mind, see if a parent who is a nurse or doctor is interested in going. If so, share the medical forms with them but under strictest confidence. Caution: Taking chaperones who are older siblings in their twenties or thirties can create some interesting situations; try to take parents.

Make it clear that chaperones cannot drink while supervising students. After the students have been secured in their rooms, chaperones can meet in the hotel bar and enjoy an adult beverage but not during the day. You are not a travel agent planning everyone's dream vacation; you're all part of a school group. (*Refer to the "Chaperone Duties" section in the "Domestic Travel" chapter for additional helpful information.*)

Organization

Schedule a trip meeting for two weeks before departure. Be sure all parents understand that one parent and the student are required to attend.

Get a file box plus a CD or large-capacity flash drive for storing all of your information. A traveling file box is recommended, as you will need to carry a lot of information at your fingertips when there may not be a computer available. Things you will need to keep there include the copies of the passport photo pages, plane tickets, copies of medical insurance cards, medical forms with prescriptions, medications, and allergies listed, rooming lists, bus lists, hotel addresses and phone numbers, admission confirmation numbers, parent contact info (phone and e-mail), chaperone info and cell numbers, travel company contact info for airlines, buses, etc.

Medical forms may be available from your school system. Be sure they include food and other allergies, medications, and prescriptions being taken while on the trip, and information that pertains to special conditions the chaperones may need to be aware of. (For example, a child is diabetic and needs to have juice or candy bars with them at all times, or a student is carrying epi pens and their chaperone should also have one and know how to use it, just in case. Also, does your school system permit the chaperone to use it or must it be administered by a school employee?) Share information with the chaperone about students with medical needs or concerns, but do so in strictest confidence. Food allergies need to be communicated to the airlines if you're flying, as do preferences such as vegetarianism. Your trip planner needs to know if you have special dietary needs in your group so adjustments can be arranged for all meals.

On that same trip to China, several students were vegetarian (no problem) and two others had shrimp and peanut allergies. A Chinese native speaker made index cards in Chinese for the allergic students to present at meals, and potential problems were averted.

Though it takes longer than assigning them yourself, have students sign up in rooms of four for hotels. If there is an uneven number, find out which is less expensive—one left-over group of two, or two groups of three. If you have students in your group that no one wants to room with for whatever reason, consider housing them in the extra two-person room (one bed for each person) and storing the large instruments in that room. If taking more than one coach while sightseeing or traveling between destinations, have students sign up for which coach they will ride. Be sure you, the director, spend time on both coaches. The same is true for school administrators or staff on the trip. Bus and room assignments will hold for the entire trip. No changing!

Meals

It is important that all participants are required to attend breakfast. Find out if your hotel offers breakfast or arrange in advance for a daily breakfast buffet so that everyone finds something to eat. Announcements for the day can easily be made while everyone eats. Chaperones attend breakfast and confirm that all students in their care are present.

If lunches are on their own, be sure each participant has a packet of local currency to purchase their meals. Don't forget to figure in the exchange rate when calculating the cost of the trip.

Dinners should be arranged for everyone for the majority of days. Your trip coordinator can take care of this but be sure to encourage variety—save a little here, spend a little more there—so everyone isn't eating burgers or pizza every night. Finding places with choices is always good.

Homestay

Consider the possibility of arranging at least part of your accommodations as a homestay experience. This puts two or more students in a local house for much less money than a hotel. Some European towns participate in this kind of arrangement frequently, as it is a way for homeowners to earn money renting out their extra rooms. Homestay usually includes breakfast, a packed (bag) lunch, and dinner, but be sure to let your trip coordinator know exactly what you want. The money you save might allow for the group to experience a local restaurant meal. Also communicate food allergies and special medical issues as needed. Consider taking a small hostess gift.

Activities

Sightseeing is top on the list. Be sure you have hired coaches available for tours or trips to attractions. (In Europe, especially, calling a chartered coach a "bus" is an insult!) Hiring a tour guide to join you on your own coach is an inexpensive way to see the area to learn some of its history.

Cultural experiences are important, too. Consider giving a concert, attending a concert, or taking in some local entertainment. Try to find things that are not available at home or in the United States.

Almost every country other than ours has a unique and extended history that puts in perspective our brief 350+ years. Check out old buildings, cathedrals, castles, government buildings, ruins, etc. for insight on antiquity. Allow some time for shopping and free time for discovery (in groups) as well.

Consider making a list of sights in a central location (example: downtown London) so groups can choose to go discovering on their own.

Story: Several groups went off in downtown London with a 5-pound limit per person. They visited thrift shops and, at the end of the free time, compared their "finds" to see who found the most exotic, funniest, gaudiest, or most amazing items. Along the way they discovered a violin maker, inexpensive rides in taxis, parks, horse-mounted police, and several small boutiques and shops to explore.

Equipment

Plan to take all of the equipment you will need to perform, but see if you can rent the large percussion equipment (timpani, chimes, bass drum, etc.) abroad, as it makes travel much easier and is often less expensive. If you take your own equipment, arrange for a trailer to be towed behind the coach. The trailer can also accommodate suitcases and instruments that might not fit easily underneath the coach. Music stands, clothespins to hold music at outdoor concerts, wardrobe boxes (from a moving company), crates full of music folders—everything takes a lot of room. Be sure large stringed instruments are in hard cases even if you have to rent them before you leave.

Check with the airlines for their policy on instruments. Most will want a list with measurements and weights of all instruments going under the plane. Some will charge extra for the oversized and over-weight instruments. Be sure you budget money for this. Measure length, width, and depth, then weigh each instrument.

Packing uniforms

Putting a tuxedo and dress shoes into a suitcase that has to stay under 50 pounds is a real challenge. Consider transporting the pants and jackets, as well as dresses or skirts, in wardrobe boxes available from moving companies or in large suitcases. Put pants neatly over a pants hanger (cardboard roll) and use masking tape or blue painters tape to tape the sides of the legs together so they don't fall off the hanger in transit. Place the jacket over the hanger, button it shut, and run a piece of tape from shoulder to shoulder to hold lapels in place during travel. Skirts and dresses can be transported the same way, hung on a pants hanger with tape holding the sides together.

Alphabetize the uniforms, dividing them into a number of boxes, and make labels on the inside of the lid with names of students whose uniforms are in that box. If uniforms are hung in a wardrobe box, put duct tape over the hanger hooks to keep the hangers from falling off the hanging bar if the box is tipped. An alternative is to purchase a few inexpensive but large suitcases (or ask parents if they have one to loan) and fold the prepared tuxes and skirts, on hangers, in half before placing in the suitcase. A plastic cleaner's bag over each uniform will help them stay flat.

Assign each suitcase to a chaperone whose responsibility will be getting it off the luggage conveyor, putting it on and off the coaches, handing out and collecting those uniforms, etc. If you label each uniform suitcase with a number (1, 2, 3, etc.) students will know where to claim their uniform and where to store it for the flight home.

Packing instruments

It is logical to assume that small instruments—flute, oboe, clarinet, and some trumpets and alto saxophones—will be carry-ons or will be inside a carry-on bag. All other instruments will need to be packed prior to flying. Get several rolls of large and small bubble wrap, two-inch clear tape, and a tape gun.

Brass, saxes, and low clarinets should stuff their bells with bunched-up bubble wrap, then wrap the valve sections or keyed bodies, and fill any extra space inside the case with pieces of bubble wrap. Wrap mouthpieces, too. Close the case and put tape over the locks. (The cases may be inspected by security but they will replace the tape and it will keep cases from falling open in the hold of the aircraft.)

Woodwinds should fill empty space by lining the case with bubble wrap, placing the instrument pieces inside and closing the case.

Small percussion instruments and accessories can be bubble wrapped then put in rolling duffle bags. Consider using several that are only partially filled, otherwise these will easily top the weight maximum limit. Be sure to protect the little instruments—triangles, woodblocks tambourines, etc. by wrapping them. Include a few new rolls of tape for the return flight.

The maximum weight is usually 50 pounds per checked instrument. Personal suitcases, too, must be under 50 pounds. To weigh, stand on the scale holding your suitcase. Then stand on the scale without the suitcase. Subtract the second weight from the first. If it is very close, consider moving a heavy item to your carry-on.

Suitcases

Everyone can take one suitcase and one carry-on, but their carry-on might be their instrument if it is small enough. Check with your airlines for the measurements. It's often a total of 24 inches, L+W+H. Flutes, oboes, and some clarinets might be able to fit inside a larger carry-on bag. All participants must be able to manage all of their bags and instruments in one trip. Assign percussion duffle bags to percussionists as their carry-on even though they will be checked. Assign uniform boxes or suitcases to chaperones as their carry-on. Some folks won't bring a carry-on so it all seems to work out just fine. The conductor's carry-on is the portable file box with forms, tickets, lists, etc.

Packing list

Distribute a suggested packing list. Include things like comfortable shoes, sunscreen, camera, electricity converters (if needed), phone chargers, any special clothing needed for an event or dinner. Remind them that there is a dress code (the nicer they look, the better they will be treated). Consider forbidding torn clothing, sweats, even blue jeans (though other colored jeans are often fine) and encouraging khakis, cords, and skirts. This will set your group apart from other student groups. List uniform parts not being transported by chaperones, plus music, mutes, extra reeds, and accessories.

A story: Believe it or not, on a trip to the Bahamas a horn player opened his case at the first concert and realized he'd forgotten his mouthpiece. Fortunately, another horn player had recently bought a new mouthpiece and still had the old one in her case. It's nice to be lucky!

The final countdown

Three weeks prior to departure

Be sure everyone has a passport. There's still time for an expedited one at increased cost. Each chaperone needs one as well. It is no longer possible for a spouse to travel under her husband's passport. If your school system required background checks or fingerprinting for overnight chaperones, be sure this is completed by all who are participating.

Notify the bank in your area that you will need foreign currency and in what amounts. They may not be able to provide you with coinage, and everything may need to be in larger bills. If this is the case, encourage students to purchase a small item once you arrive in the airport—a pack of gum or mints, perhaps—so they have smaller currency and coins available. In some countries, public rest rooms may require the purchase of toilet paper or have pay toilets. It's better to be prepared.

Get $500–$1,000 or more, depending on the length of your trip, in foreign currency to carry as emergency cash. You may also want to have some US dollars in emergency cash as well. Examples of why you might need this include: students who bring a bank card that won't work, emergency medical expenses, emergency taxi rides, money to change the ticket of anyone who is very ill and must be sent home, tips for coach drivers, hotel maids, and tour guides, eventual purchase of small gifts for chaperones. Keep receipts for everything spent.

Ask a parent to research the best options for students to access spending money in your destination. Traveler's checks, bank cards with PIN numbers, carrying U.S. cash—each has a fee involved. Is it better to get traveler's checks in the currency of your destination or carry cash and pay the conversion fees? Ask that parent to make a brief presentation at the upcoming trip meeting.

Three weeks before departure hand out historical or other interesting background information about the places you'll be visiting. List websites or guidebooks that you think are useful. Encourage students to do their own research. Hang travel posters or maps of your destination on a wall in your room. Check out and share related books from the library.

Two weeks prior to departure

Hold a trip meeting. Require that at least one parent in every family attend. Chaperones and any school staff who are going should also be there. It is important for parents to meet the chaperones and for you to have the opportunity to address everyone. Consider having documents prepared that need signatures at this meeting: a list of rules for students and parents to sign, a release form releasing you, the school staff, and chaperones of any responsibility for actions taken by students who are not under your direct supervision or are supposed to be asleep (for example, at night, once they're taped into their rooms and they decide to drink all the booze they secretly bought that day and end up breaking things in the hotel room, or when they decide to climb the outside balconies to visit the students in the room upstairs). Rules should be few and simple, and align with the school system' expectations. Having students and parents sign a document that says they know they will be sent home at the parents' expense for violation of curfew carries a lot of weight. There must be consequences for rule-breaking. Being ten minutes late getting back to the coach after free time warrants a smaller consequence but an action nonetheless. Plan for this!

Another story: The four students in a hotel room across from the pool decided, at midnight, that they would exit via their untaped patio door, run to the pool, dive in, swim across, get out, and run back to their room without getting caught. Unknown to them was the fact that the pool had been shocked with chlorine after it closed at 11 p.m. They would have gotten away with it except that they all needed medical attention and eye wash from the very strong chlorine treatment. They spent the next day, which was at an amusement park, sitting in the food court with a variety of chaperones, serving "detention" for breaking the rules.

Consider the fact that you may have students participating who have never been away from home for several days (or more), or that some may have never flown. Partner them with a more experienced traveler and make sure there are games and other diversions, especially during takeoff and landing. Having someone explain what's going to happen will put them more at ease. If you are traveling to a country with different customs, be sure to have an orientation at the trip meeting so all know what to expect and what is unacceptable.

Many students were surprised by the lack of toilets in China. However, a student on the trip who had spent quite a bit of time in India had explained to all how to use the hole in the floor.

One week prior to departure

Check with the airlines to be sure they have all that they need from you. If possible, offer to bring the instruments to the airport earlier in the day or the day before departure. It may guarantee that all your instruments are at the destination when you arrive.

Have a parent pick up the currency at the bank and put it in small envelopes with each participant's name. Keep envelopes in a safe place until the day of travel.

Call or check on line for the procedure for replacing a lost passport overseas.

Doublecheck with the coach company to be sure everything is set.

Cell phones often require special settings to work overseas. Assign someone to research this and identify the best way(s) for students to stay in touch with parents. (If cell use is very expensive, consider buying a travel plan for one student who will call home every night with the daily update that can then be sent to all parents via e-mail.) Prepaid phone cards may be another option depending on the country.

Finalize all lists; be sure all forms are collected. Read through the medical forms so you know what you're dealing with in terms of specific needs. Share with the nurse/doctor, if you have one going. Share important information with the specific chaperone of the student with medical needs. Medical information must be treated confidentially.

Strongly consider taking coaches to the airport to guarantee that everyone arrives in plenty of time (2.5–3 hours early, as it takes longer to check in a group). However, to save money, consider having parents meet students at the airport for the return trip. If the airport is further than an hour or so away, it's probably best to arrange for buses to make the return trip to school. Include these fees in your trip price.

On a trip to England, the buses were loaded and waiting in the school parking lot for one student who had not arrived. Since it was in the days before cell phones, no call could be made. Finally, the bus left, leaving behind a chaperone with a car. When the student arrived, the chaperone drove to the airport, where the tardy instrumentalist joined the group. Meanwhile all the others had cleared security and could relax with time to spare. The tardy student's parents paid the airport parking for the chaperone.

Line up a half-dozen parents to help load suitcases and instruments under the coaches on departure day.

Assure all students that it is your intention that everyone has a safe and enjoyable trip but that you will tolerate no funny business. If you have developed the kind of rapport with your students that allows you to feel comfortable taking them out of the country, you're in good shape. If you are taking this trip to have fun and look the other way while they have fun, remember that parents are entrusting you with their most precious possessions and that they expect you to be responsible for keeping them safe. The release form does not protect you from irresponsible behavior.

Explain to the students what they should expect when going through customs.

The day before departure

Be sure all of *your* things are ready. Get tickets and money packets out of the safe and put them in your carry-on. Be sure you have attendance lists for the parents assigned as bus monitors.

Reiterate what students need to bring: suitcase, instrument, music, accessories, a bag lunch, whatever.

The day of departure

Allow plenty of time to pack the instruments, label all suitcases and instruments (consider a brightly colored paper tag with the school name and the addresses and dates of your hotel stays in case a suitcase gets misplaced and the airlines has to find you after you've changed cities). Also, label all suitcase and instrument handles with brightly colored tape to identify it as belonging to the group. This will be helpful in the airport baggage claim area. Load the buses. Suitcases and instruments take a lot of room and must be packed carefully underneath the coach. Small instruments should go in the overhead racks inside the bus.

Do a passport check before leaving the school parking lot.

Allow several hours to get through security. Instruments will likely be inspected (which is why it's helpful to take the large instruments to the airport the day before), and moving a group of students takes more time than you'd think.

Don't wait more than ten minutes for anyone who doesn't make it to the departure point on time. Leave a chaperone behind with their car to bring the tardy student(s) once they arrive. You'll need to pay their airport parking but, meanwhile, the rest of the group will get checked in.

Plane tickets are issued from your alphabetical list, therefore students and chaperones will likely be seated alphabetically. It's easiest if everyone gets on the plane with their own ticket and sits in their own seat. When the seat belt sign is removed, students can switch seats fairly easily without disturbing others on the plane. However, anyone with a special meal request will need to be in their assigned seat for meals.

Once the plane takes off and you know that everyone is on board, allow yourself a few moments to sit and relax. Your work isn't done, but for the next several hours, they're all safe and in one place. This is a good time to pass out info to chaperones and hand out money packets. (Get everyone to initial a payment sheet saying that they received their money. Your bookkeeper at school may need this for the auditor.)

Read through the itinerary and be sure you and each of the chaperones has some free time with no responsibilities. If the entire group has a chunk of time for exploring and shopping, this counts for them as well. Being on duty 24/7 is not a realistic expectation for anyone (except you).

Decide whether you will collect passports from the students once they've cleared arrival at the destination. Keep passports with the group (in your travel file) in case there is a need, but the chance of anyone losing theirs is much less if they are in the care of an adult. Another option is to have each chaperone carry the passports for the students in their charge.

Planning for the unexpected

▶ *On a trip to Bermuda, students over sixteen were allowed, with special parental permission and extra insurance, to rent a moped and travel around the island. Because the roads were damp, one moped turned a corner too fast and the boys went down, sliding with bare skin on the coral-paved roads. Bermuda's coral is full of tiny micro-organisms that don't affect the natives but cause havoc for nonresidents. The hotel manager* said that the best solution was to walk into the sea and let the salt water cleanse the big scrapes. It was February and the sea was quite cold. The screams from the boys as they walked in waist-deep could be heard all the way back at the hotel. But the manager was right. The road rash healed nicely, and everyone drove more carefully for the next few days.

▶ On a trip to England, a parent chaperone cancelled just before the trip because his wife's illness had taken a bad turn and he'd decided to stay home. Another parent bought his tickets and paid fees to transfer the tickets. The morning after we arrived in London, a call came that the mother, after an extended illness, had passed and the family wanted the son to come home. One of the chaperones, a staff member with extensive travel experience, took the young man in a taxi, emergency cash in hand, and finagled him onto an oversold plane home. Having a chaperone on hand who could facilitate that was truly amazing.

▶ At trip meetings, parents always asked why certain restrictions were on the Rules List. The one that brought the most interest was "No permanent alterations to your body may be made while on this trip. This includes tattoos, body piercings, etc." While on a trip to Mexico, a student decided to get his tongue pierced. It was quite inexpensive at the Mexican market where students were given free time to walk around and shop. However, everyone considered him quite lucky that he did not contract any diseases from the needle. Three months later, he let the hole close and heal.

▶ One tour guide in Amsterdam surprised the group by taking the coach through the "Red Light District" and explaining that the live models in the store windows were actually for sale "by the hour." Fortunately, Amsterdam had many other interesting sights much closer to the hotel!

▶ Check the weather reports for your destination before you go. One trip to a music festival in Holland had the group staying in a seaside town where the daily temperatures were in the low 40s but the wind chill kept it just barely above freezing. It would have been manageable except for the one-mile walk from the hotel to breakfast each morning then back to the hotel before the day's activities began. Warmer coats plus hats, scarves, and gloves would have been welcomed.

▶ The day of departure arrived for a trip to China. One young man, who had been perfectly fine the day before, showed up on crutches with a *swollen ankle. Adjustments had to be made for others to transport his suitcase and instrument and carry-on everywhere the group went. Emergency cash was used to rent a wheelchair on days when there was a lot of walking.*

▶ *On that same trip to China, the dinner hour following the last joint concert was spent repacking all the percussion and instruments for the flight home the next morning. Other ensembles went on to dinner and, by the time the instruments were packed, the group was extremely tired and hungry. Emergency cash was used to arrange for pizza and sodas at the hotel. It was the perfect end to a trip. Who knew there would be a Papa John's one block from the hotel in Beijing! When the other groups returned from their dinner, they were all clutching their stomachs and complaining that the food was bad and they were all sick. Staying behind to pack for morning departure really paid off!*

▶ *On a trip to the Bahamas, one suitcase did not arrive with the rest of the luggage. It was promised in two days' time. Emergency cash was used to purchase shorts and shirts for the young man who was clever enough to pack his swimsuit and some underwear in his carry-on.*

▶ *While in Bermuda, the groups were disappointed because there were no other bands or choirs there but ours. The festival performances, while good, were not driven by the added edge of friendly competition. Then news reached them of a huge snow storm up the entire east coast, closing all airports. Snowed out! Might not be able to fly home on time! Jetsetters flying home from Belize and Aruba being diverted to Bermuda because of closed airports! Total attitude change! And then word that the airports were open again and flights would leave on schedule. Sigh! The emotional roller coaster! So the jazz band played a dance in the hotel for the waylaid guests, and emergency cash was used to purchase refreshments for the student "party." Of course, Bermuda, being an island, was a very expensive place to buy sodas and chips—about ten times the normal prices.*

▶ *Lesson learned from a trip to a music festival in Williamsburg: The band was wearing red band tee-shirts so they could be easily recognized by chaperones and seen from a distance. Then the rain began and most folks ran inside to buy a rain poncho. Suddenly, everyone in the park was wearing the same yellow poncho. On a later trip, it was suggested that everyone bring a clear rain poncho so the matching shirts were still visible.*

You'll notice that all of these stories have something in common: everything was unexpected and unplanned. These kinds of situations are always simmering. When they erupt, be sure you stay calm and make good decisions. You've spent way too much time planning the trip to go home angry or disappointed at the end of it!

Matching shirts are a great idea for days spent in an amusement park or with free time, in groups, for exploring an historical city, especially because chaperones who don't know everyone can easily recognize group members. Find a local business (music store?) to pay for the shirts in return for their ad on the back of the shirt or in your concert programs back home.

The inevitable misplaced passport

This is a serious problem. Consider having passport checks every time you get on a coach to go somewhere else. Or, as mentioned earlier, have chaperones hold the passports for the students in their charge or let the director carry all of the passports.

However, since passports have to be used as ID when using traveler's checks, there will be times when students need to carry them and risk losing them.

This is why copies of the photo page are so important. Have the assigned chaperone take the student and the copied passport page to the American embassy. With the computer age in full swing, it may be possible to do all of this via fax and e-mail from the hotel. Explain the situation and give the date and time of your departure home, plus the airline and flight number. Hopefully, the missing document will be discovered in enough time to leave with the rest of the group, however, it's best to be prepared. No one at the airport can give permission to board without a passport, and it is impossible to travel between countries without one.

The importance of delegating

You have spent a lot of time and energy planning and executing all the preparations for the trip. Allow yourself some time to enjoy yourself and be with the students, and let the chaperones help you. If chaperones are assigned to specific rooms of students, they are responsible for that group. If someone in the group gets sick and stays behind in the hotel that day, the assigned chaperone stays with them and another chaperone keeps track of the remaining students for the day. If someone loses a passport, the assigned chaperone takes care of the procedure to find it or get permission to return home. You stay near or with the majority of the group. ■

FINAL NOTE

Those of us who are passionate about music teach because we want others to experience the rewards of music making. In our academic preparation, we hone our performance skills, we study scores and conducting, we study music history, and we learn theory. These are all critical. However, university music education programs cannot possibly teach us everything we need to know. Being a successful music educator is also about learning how to most effectively transmit our knowledge to our students and build an environment that provides fertile ground for learning and expansion. Our success also depends on effective marketing, administration, promotion, fundraising, and hundreds of other nonmusical and sometimes tedious activities. The nonmusical list sometimes feels too long and can overwhelm us.

I wrote this book to prevent teachers from having to reinvent the wheel, even though that's what most of us do every day. I want to help teachers feel *less* overwhelmed and *more* rewarded. The ideas here are intended to encourage newer teachers to think beyond their textbooks, and to nudge experienced teachers to try new techniques or think of old techniques in new ways. The artistic and practical resources here are presented to help you expand your knowledge and stay on top of your game.

Thank you for allowing me to share all of this with you. I encourage each of you to share with your colleagues the techniques and ideas that work for you. In the end, our hard work, our struggles, and also our joys are about one thing: providing meaningful musical experiences for our students. ■

APPENDIX

Quotes that Inspire

"Perfection is not attainable, but if we chase perfection we can often find excellence."

—Vince Lombardi

"In terms of brain development, musical performance is every bit as important educationally as reading or writing."

—Oliver Sacks, British neurologist

"If you practice, you get better.
If you get better, you play with better players.
If you play with better players, you play better music.
If you play better music, you have more fun.
If you have fun, you want to practice more.
If you practice more, you get better . . ."

—Doug Yeo, professional bass trombonist

"Courage doesn't always roar. Sometimes it is the quiet voice at the end of the day saying 'I will try again tomorrow.'"

—Mary Ann Radmacher

"It occurred to me by intuition, and music was the driving force behind that intuition. My discovery was the result of musical perception."

—Albert Einstein, in speaking of his Theory of Relativity

"Inaction rarely leads to accomplishments."
—UNKNOWN

"A ship in the harbor is safe—but that's not what ships are for."
—JOHN A. SHEDD

"Music is a higher revelation than all wisdom and philosophy."
—LUDWIG VAN BEETHOVEN

"Intonation matters! Don't just hit the target, hit the bullseye."
—UNKNOWN

"Never rest while playing music.
You either play silences during which you listen,
or you play sounds during which you listen."
—UNKNOWN

"If you can hear yourself you are:
1) too loud, 2) not blending, 3) not in tune."
—UNKNOWN

"Three parts of a good sound: *start* the note (tip of the tongue); *sustain* the note (back of the tongue); *release* the note (air in the throat)."
—UNKNOWN

"Caring about others, running the risk of feeling, and leaving an impact on people, brings happiness."
—HAROLD KUSHNER, AUTHOR

"People can say they care but it means nothing until they prove it."
—UNKNOWN

"Never stop doing little things for others. Sometimes those little things occupy the bigger part of the heart."
—UNKNOWN

"Too often we underestimate the power of a touch, a smile, a kind word, a listening ear, an honest compliment, or the smallest act of caring, all of which have the potential to turn a life around."
—LEO BUSCAGLIA

"Everybody—even monsters—needed a little attention once in a while."
—RICK RIORDEN

"Never be so busy as not to think of others."
—MOTHER TERESA

"Excellence is the result of caring more than others think is wise, risking more than others think is safe, dreaming more than others think is practical, and expecting more than others think is possible."
—RONNIE OLDHAM

"To play a wrong note is insignificant. To play without passion is inexcusable."
—LUDWIG VAN BEETHOVEN

"Kindness can transform someone's dark moment with a blaze of light. You'll never know how much your caring matters. Make a difference for another today."
—AMY LEIGH MERCEE

"I feel the capacity to care is the thing which gives life its deepest significance."
—PABLO CASALS

"The greatest musicians *aren't* the ones that play the loudest, or play the most notes, or the flashiest solos. They are the ones that play what the music calls for, are team players, and *always* make people feel something every time they play."
—WWW.MUSICIANSUNSHINE.COM

"A pessimist sees the difficulty in every opportunity. An optimist sees the opportunity in every difficulty."

—Winston Churchill

"There are only two things worth aiming for, good music and a clean conscience."

—Paul Hindemith

"Music washes away from the soul the dust of everyday life."

—Red Auerbach

"Music is a defining element of character."

—Plato

From *Mr. Holland's Opus:*
Vice Principal Wolters: I care about these kids just as much as you do. And if I'm forced to choose between Mozart and reading and writing and long division, I choose long division.
Glenn Holland: Well, I guess you can cut the arts as much as you want, Gene. Sooner or later, these kids aren't going to have anything to read or write about.

"Where words fail, music speaks."

—Hans Christian Anderson

"People who make music together cannot be enemies, at least while the music lasts."

—Paul Hindemith

"Music is the hardest kind of art. It doesn't hang up on a wall and wait to be stared at and enjoyed by passersby. It's communication. It's hours and hours being put into a work of art that may only last, in reality, for a few moments . . . but if done well, and truly appreciated, it lasts in our hearts forever. That's art. Speaking with your heart to the hearts of others."

—Dan Romano

"Be a yardstick of quality. Some people aren't used to an environment where excellence is expected."

—STEVE JOBS

"Shoot for the moon. Even if you miss, you'll land among the stars!"

—UNKNOWN

"Music is the electrical soil in which the spirit lives, thinks, and invents."

—LUDWIG VAN BEETHOVEN

"It's easy to play any musical instrument: all you have to do is touch the right key at the right time and the instrument will play itself."

—J.S. BACH

"Music expresses that which cannot be put into words and that which cannot remain silent."

—VICTOR HUGO

"Band prepares you for life."

—RICHARD SAUCEDO

ABOUT THE AUTHOR

Sally S. Wagner retired after forty years of public school teaching, thirty-seven as a high school director, and the last thirty-four as Director of Bands at Eleanor Roosevelt High School in Greenbelt, Maryland, where she conducted four concert bands and jazz band, and oversaw the Dixieland Combo and several chamber ensembles. During her years at the school her bands earned a reputation for superior musicianship and performance standards, and were recognized as outstanding by respected adjudicators at local, national, and international music festivals.

Ms. Wagner earned degrees from Michigan State University and the University of Delaware. She is a member of the National Association for Music Education, National Band Association, Women Band Directors International, and Maryland Band Directors Association. She is active as a clinician and guest conductor, and has articles published in *The Woman Conductor, BandWorld*, and *The Instrumentalist*. She adjudicates local, state, national, and international music festivals. In addition to writing *The Pursuit of Excellence: A Band Director's Guide to Success,* she is coauthor, with David Fedderly, of *Brass Instruments: Purchasing, Maintenance, Troubleshooting, and More* (Meredith Music Publications).